THE FIFTH SUMMIT OF THE ASIA PACIFIC ECONOMIC COOPERATION FORUM

AF770889

HEARING

BEFORE THE

SUBCOMMITTEE ON
ASIA AND THE PACIFIC

OF THE

COMMITTEE ON
INTERNATIONAL RELATIONS
HOUSE OF REPRESENTATIVES

ONE HUNDRED FIFTH CONGRESS

FIRST SESSION

NOVEMBER 6, 1997

Printed for the use of the Committee on International Relations

U.S. GOVERNMENT PRINTING OFFICE
47–149 CC WASHINGTON : 1998

For sale by the U.S. Government Printing Office
Superintendent of Documents, Congressional Sales Office, Washington, DC 20402
ISBN 0-16-056391-7

COMMITTEE ON INTERNATIONAL RELATIONS

BENJAMIN A. GILMAN, New York, *Chairman*

WILLIAM GOODLING, Pennsylvania
JAMES A. LEACH, Iowa
HENRY J. HYDE, Illinois
DOUG BEREUTER, Nebraska
CHRISTOPHER SMITH, New Jersey
DAN BURTON, Indiana
ELTON GALLEGLY, California
ILEANA ROS-LEHTINEN, Florida
CASS BALLENGER, North Carolina
DANA ROHRABACHER, California
DONALD A. MANZULLO, Illinois
EDWARD R. ROYCE, California
PETER T. KING, New York
JAY KIM, California
STEVEN J. CHABOT, Ohio
MARSHALL "MARK" SANFORD, South Carolina
MATT SALMON, Arizona
AMO HOUGHTON, New York
TOM CAMPBELL, California
JON FOX, Pennsylvania
LINDSEY O. GRAHAM, South Carolina
JOHN McHUGH, New York
ROY BLUNT, Missouri
KEVIN BRADY, Texas

LEE HAMILTON, Indiana
SAM GEJDENSON, Connecticut
TOM LANTOS, California
HOWARD BERMAN, California
GARY ACKERMAN, New York
ENI F.H. FALEOMAVAEGA, American Samoa
MATTHEW G. MARTINEZ, California
DONALD M. PAYNE, New Jersey
ROBERT ANDREWS, New Jersey
ROBERT MENENDEZ, New Jersey
SHERROD BROWN, Ohio
CYNTHIA A. McKINNEY, Georgia
ALCEE L. HASTINGS, Florida
PAT DANNER, Missouri
EARL HILLIARD, Alabama
BRAD SHERMAN, California
ROBERT WEXLER, Florida
STEVE ROTHMAN, New Jersey
BOB CLEMENT, Tennessee
BILL LUTHER, Minnesota
JIM DAVIS, Florida

RICHARD J. GARON, *Chief of Staff*
MICHAEL H. VAN DUSEN, *Democratic Chief of Staff*

SUBCOMMITTEE ON ASIA AND THE PACIFIC

DOUG BEREUTER, Nebraska, *Chairman*

JAMES A. LEACH, Iowa
DANA ROHRABACHER, California
PETER T. KING, New York
JAY KIM, California
MATT SALMON, Arizona
JON FOX, Pennsylvania
JOHN M. McHUGH, New York
DONALD A. MANZULLO, Illinois
EDWARD R. ROYCE, California

HOWARD L. BERMAN, California
ENI F.H. FALEOMAVAEGA, American Samoa
ROBERT E. ANDREWS, New Jersey
SHERROD BROWN, Ohio
MATTHEW G. MARTINEZ, California
ALCEE L. HASTINGS, Florida
WALTER H. CAPPS, California
ROBERT WEXLER, Florida

MIKE ENNIS, *Subcommittee Staff Director*
RICHARD KESSLER, *Democratic Professional Staff Member*
DAN MARTZ, *Counsel*
HEIDI L. HENNIG, *Staff Associate*

CONTENTS

WITNESSES

APPENDIX

THE FIFTH SUMMIT OF THE ASIA PACIFIC ECONOMIC COOPERATION FORUM

THURSDAY, NOVEMBER 6, 1997

HOUSE OF REPRESENTATIVES,
SUBCOMMITTEE ON ASIA AND THE PACIFIC,
COMMITTEE ON INTERNATIONAL RELATIONS,
Washington, DC.

The Subcommittee met, pursuant to notice, at 1:50 p.m. in room 2172, Rayburn House Office Building, Hon. Doug Bereuter (chairman of the Subcommittee) presiding.

Mr. BEREUTER. The Subcommittee on Asia and the Pacific will come to order.

Today's hearing focuses on the Fifth Summit of the Asia Pacific Economic Corporation Forum. We will shortly have a competing hearing in one of the subcommittees of the International Relations Committee on fast track, and today is a hectic day with lots of parliamentary and procedural interruptions. It happens every year during the last week of the session.

I am very interested in having more information conveyed to the American public, as well as my colleagues, about APEC and its operations. As I said, today's hearing does focus on the Fifth Summit of the Asia Pacific Economic Corporation Forum. I open the hearing with skeptical optimism regarding APEC's future to serve as an agent of economic growth in the region through their reduction of trade and investment barriers.

Overall, APEC has been a very valuable initiative and multilateral initiative. The Clinton Administration and the President himself have played a very important role in making it a viable and more important organization all the time. In 1994, the APEC Heads of State met in Bogor, Indonesia. There they made the remarkable commitment of free trade and investment among the 18 APEC members by the year 2010 for the industrialized countries and the year 2020 for the rest of the members. The Bogor Declaration implies that after 2020, the U.S. Congress will no longer have to debate extending most-favored-nation status or normal tariff status to China because tariff rates between the two countries will be zero. It holds out the hope that companies that want to establish subsidiaries in any APEC country can focus their attention on the economics of the investment and not on the difficulties and the corruptive practices very often necessary for bureaucratic approval.

Positive steps to move the process forward have been made. They were achieved, for example, at the 1996 meeting in the Philippines where most members tabled credible, but nonetheless uneven, individual action plans. Additionally, APEC demonstrated its flexibility as an action-forcing event by launching support for the Information Technology Agreement (the ITA). Nevertheless, there are differences between APEC member countries.

At the 1995 Osaka APEC meetings some APEC members such as Japan, China, the Republic of Korea and Taiwan, sought to frustrate the implementation of the Bogor commitment by requesting flexibility in the implementation of trade liberalization for sensitive sectors, such as agriculture. At least it seemed like that was their intent.

Another major challenge is that certain countries have no history of bilaterally negotiating free trade with one another. When such countries reach the point where their concessions go beyond those agreed to under the World Trade Organization or other agreements, they are likely to encounter strong political resistance. Is Japan or the Republic of Korea willing to open its rice markets to free imports from the United States and Thailand by the year 2010? Therefore, APEC's capability to induce its members to commit to such difficult economic agreements will be the true test of its viability as an international trade organization capable of securing economic growth throughout the region.

There can be no doubt that a breakdown or stalemate in the APEC trade and investment liberalization process would be extremely harmful to U.S. interests. The Clinton Administration strongly supports APEC and has hailed it as being the cornerstone of its economic policy in the region. In order for President Clinton and the U.S. negotiators to safeguard U.S. economic interests and take the lead in trade liberalization efforts at the APEC meeting this month, it is critical that President Clinton be given fast track authority. This measure was supported by a surprisingly wide margin in the Senate, and I encourage my colleagues in the House to do the same.

This is not to say that the route toward free trade will not be difficult. It will, as we in the Congress learned well from the bruising battle over NAFTA approval. Problems such as rising trade deficits and the potential of nontariff barriers faced by American exporters are real issues which will need strong action. Still, the vision of free trade is there.

As one of the most open economies of the world, we stand to benefit the most from further trade and liberalization activities and investment as well. I hope this Administration's stated policy of encouraging bilateral free trade agreements in the region and the President's belated lobbying for fast track legislation do indicate a real desire and commitment by the United States to continue to be a champion for trade liberalization in APEC and other fora. I think it is a legitimate indication.

One of the issues we will be examining during this afternoon's hearing, among other subjects, is whether or not APEC should create a fund to assist in future economic crises in the region.

I am pleased to introduce our four witnesses for today's hearings, two panels of witnesses, all with solid backgrounds and knowledge of APEC's past history and future goals.

On our first panel, we are very delighted to have the Honorable John Wolf, Department of State Coordinator for APEC. Mr. Wolf is a career foreign service officer, confirmed as ambassador to APEC in February 1997.

The second panel includes an excellent and diverse panel of academic and commercial representatives who are very knowledgeable about APEC. It includes Mr. Robert Denham, CEO of Salomon Incorporated and U.S. representative to the APEC Business Advisory Council; the Honorable Bennett Johnston, currently president of the U.S.-PECC and the former senior Senator from Louisiana, who has a long and demonstrated strong history and knowledgeable interest, in the Asia Pacific region; and Dr. C. Fred Bergsten—I would say Mr. APEC in the United States—that is what I call him—director of the Institute for International Economics and former chairman of the Eminent Persons Group (EPG), of the APEC throughout EPG's existence from 1993 to 1995.

We will have plenty of interruptions, I am afraid, after the first hour. I would ask the witnesses if they would limit their remarks to about 5 to 8 minutes, if at all possible, so that we can cope with the House's erratic schedule today. When the Ranking Member or his designee arrives, I will interrupt and permit them to introduce a statement or deliver it orally.

Welcome to the Subcommittee. I wish we had a full membership here, but what you say will be picked up and heard by a wide audience. I will learn from what you have to say, I am sure, as we all will. Please proceed as you wish.

STATEMENT OF AMBASSADOR JOHN S. WOLF, U.S. COORDINATOR FOR THE ASIA PACIFIC ECONOMIC COOPERATION FORUM

Ambassador WOLF. Mr. Chairman, thank you for the invitation. Thank you for the support you have given to us on APEC and for the support that you have made so clear on fast track. I will try to do nothing that slows the House down in its progress. A few remarks, though, from my written statement.

Some would ask, why discuss APEC now? When the hot issues in the region and even globally appear to be finance and currency instability and not economic cooperation, why?

Why? Because we care about the stability of the Asia Pacific. We care about the millions of Americans who are of Asian and Pacific descent, and because thousands of U.S. companies are involved in the region and because millions of U.S. jobs depend on Asia's well-being.

In his first term, President Clinton set forth a vision of a Pacific community based on a mutually reinforcing framework of shared strength, shared prosperity and shared commitment to democratic values. APEC is the premier multilateral forum for advancing those policies. Up to this point, APEC's efforts have worked on two sides of the issues, building the marketplaces of the Asia Pacific while at the same time opening those marketplaces. That, incidentally, is why tomorrow's vote on fast track is so important. The vote is about the ability of U.S. firms to compete abroad. It is about America's ability to continue the leadership which we have provided to the global trade and financial system for over 50 years.

There are important negotiations ahead in the World Trade Organization, important opportunities to push sectoral liberalization through APEC, and none of these will go forward without that authority. Events of the past few weeks have made clear our economic interests are intertwined with those of Asia. We need the flexibility and the authority to continue our leadership.

What we must ask ourselves on fast track is, are we going to lead as the rules are made or are we going to sit back and let others, who do not share our interests, make them for us?

This year, APEC leaders in Vancouver will have to confront today's immediate issues, issues related to how the region's economies can adjust to their recent economic difficulties, pursue necessary reform and get back on the path of strong, sustainable economic growth. We are working on six sets of issues as we go toward that meeting.

First, we expect that Asia's financial crisis will be at the top of many leaders' agendas. We have been making extraordinary efforts to help the countries of the region address the complex economic issues we are all reading about daily. Our involvement in support of the IMF program for Indonesia is a visible sign of that interest. Finance officials in the APEC region are looking at how APEC can help to promote or to restore financial stability in Asia, but no one should imagine that there will be some silver bullet that comes from the November leaders' meeting. Improvement requires a steadfast commitment to sound policies and demonstrated efforts to adjust.

Second, APEC is in the process of identifying sectors for early voluntary sectoral liberalization. We want an outcome that is commercially significant and one that helps increase the attractiveness of projects in Asia. Infrastructure-related goods and services, where Americans are the leaders in providing goods and services, fit this specification exactly.

Third, we want to use APEC to clear the trade underbrush. New air express techniques to speed goods to customers and a mutual recognition agreement in telecommunications to eliminate needless retesting of equipment are two examples of what we are doing and what we need to do more of.

APEC is not a traditional trade organization. We do not spend our time in mind-numbing negotiations. Our work is aimed at focused outcomes that increase efficiency and assure more and better jobs, safer workplaces and a cleaner environment. And for this work, APEC cannot depend just on government officials; there must be an active involvement from the private sector. That is why your second panel is so important. Their ideas have been a valuable contribution.

Much of our work focuses on APEC's economic and technical cooperation. If we get the architecture right, businesses will be able to take advantage of the opportunities and our economies will grow.

We want to support the President's economic commerce initiative. There it is the private sector that needs to provide the leadership. We believe the government should intervene only minimally to create a stable environment for economic commerce.

Fifth is an issue right out of today's headlines. It is the environmental issues. These are issues that face us all, on which we all need to act together.

APEC is about building a community. It is a first step, but it is the soundness of this community and the commitment of its members to work together, to share in the security, the prosperity and the values that the community has to offer. It is this that will keep the economic dynamism of the Asia Pacific region alive and expand it for all the world to share. The Pacific community is real and the United States will continue to be a vital part of it.

Thank you for having this hearing and giving us an opportunity to discuss the issues that are important to all of us.

[The prepared statement of Ambassador Wolf appears in the appendix.]

Mr. BEREUTER. Thank you for your summary, Ambassador.

I would like to begin by asking you about the proposal that apparently will be under consideration at the Vancouver summit which would create—I don't know if I should use the phrase, but it is typically called a "bailout fund," to offer economic assistance to member countries in the future. It is my understanding that the U.S. position is negative or at least not positive.

Australia, I think, has that position. What are the reasons for the U.S. position? How do you think it fits with the IMF? Is the fact that the IMF is available for what appears to be the same purposes a major factor in any decision that has been made, at least tentatively, on the part of our government?

Ambassador WOLF. Mr. Chairman, I think if you described it as a "bailout fund," there is clearly no question, we oppose. Nor do we think that the IMF is that. We think that whatever financial arrangements are made, it will be important for the International Monetary Fund (IMF) to be at the center.

There are lots of ideas at play, lots of discussions among the financial authorities in the region. I am not the expert, but I do know that their discussions have focused all through the region on the centrality of an IMF role. The reason for this is very clear. We have learned the lesson, after Mexico, time after time. It is important to assure that even when countries receive funds from outside financial sources, from other countries, for instance, that these resources will be used in support of an adjustment program that supports the necessary measures to restore financial stability, and we believe that the IMF is best positioned to assure a credible adjustment program. Adequate resources are important, but it is sound macroeconomic policies that are a sine qua non. IMF, we believe it is important. It is important for the IMF to have sufficient resources. It is important for it to have flexibility to respond quickly and efficiently. These are a number of the issues that the treasuries are in the process of discussing and which they will discuss at a meeting of financial officials from the APEC region in mid-November.

Mr. BEREUTER. Who are the primary proponents of the proposal that may be subject to deliberation in Vancouver?

Ambassador WOLF. Mr. Chairman, as I say, there are a number of different ideas out there. There was an idea that was, I suppose, originally from Japan that was for a freestanding fund that was completely removed from the IMF. Several of the ASEAN countries have indicated that they would be interested in some kind of a facility that would have funds additional to the IMF, but whose disbursement would be dependent on an IMF program.

Dr. Bergsten has been very active in terms of proposing a variety of ideas. I think I will leave it to him to discuss his ideas.

As I say, there are a lot of discussions, there are a lot of ideas. We believe that it is absolutely essential that the IMF be at the center of whatever efforts take place.

Mr. BEREUTER. Fair enough. Ambassador, there was a proposal to ease visa restrictions on APEC business travelers. What is the position of our government? What is the status of that proposal? Do you expect it will be actively discussed or potentially brought to action in Vancouver?

Ambassador WOLF. That is a part of the Business Advisory Council's recommendation, and this year they will be proposing three options. One option will have to do with visa-free travel. Another will have to do with the travel card. The third would be for 5-year multiple-entry visas.

We currently do 10-year multiple-entry visas for most of the countries in the Asia Pacific. Four or five economies are working on the travel card. The visa-free travel idea is not getting real far, but if I might, I believe that what I hear all around the region from American companies, from the Asia Pacific Council of American Chambers of Commerce is that the core issue for them in terms of business mobility is actually the issue of moving people within their companies. When they are established in one country and they want to move people, whether they are Singaporeans or Americans or whatever, to a meeting to do a temporary project or to do a longer stay in a management capacity, the work permit issues are really the big ones; and in our view, we are looking for ways to establish some performance criteria by which countries that want to be attractive can do things that cut costs dramatically by cutting down the time, the number of forms and the fees that are required for that kind of mobility.

Mr. BEREUTER. Does our government recognize the legitimacy of the concerns that are raised by the business groups about the visa and about facilitating travel?

Ambassador WOLF. Yes, sir. We, for instance, are working on this in a variety of ways. We have extended 10-year multiple-entry visas to most of the APEC economies, I think 15 of the other 17. We are working on ways—INS has things like the INS pass program, which is designed to allow frequent travelers to the United States to swipe a card and match a handprint against a registered handprint, and by those means, to improve movement through immigration.

There is another side of it, as well, which is the whole question of the Customs area, getting the bags on the carousel and getting it out of the Customs area. All of those things are areas where the transportation working group and the group on business mobility are actively engaged.

Mr. BEREUTER. I don't know if this is the area where we ought to seek action, but it seems to me that it would be good if there were specific, concrete achievements coming out of APEC that relate to business, that are more than important in principle, but something very tangible.

Ambassador WOLF. I agree with you. We are working with the other economies. I hope they would be as flexible on visas as we are. We think that there are a number of economies where American business and Americans who work abroad provide services for infrastructure, for the building of infrastructure projects, for instance, where we can do things that make it a lot easier for people to get there and enable us to be much more competitive because of that. That is another place where we want to focus on very specific outcomes—shorter times, fewer forms, lower fees.

Mr. BEREUTER. Moving to a much different plane, important in both cases, you and I both mentioned fast track and its importance. At what point in the APEC process, specifically, do you consider fast track authority to be essential?

Ambassador WOLF. Tomorrow.

Mr. BEREUTER. That is a good general answer.

When is it that you will come up against the wall and you can no longer make any progress because you lack the authorization from Congress for the President to proceed with negotiations?

Ambassador WOLF. We are there now, Mr. Chairman. We are in the process of looking at early voluntary sector liberalization. In May, APEC trade ministers asked senior officials to identify, asked economies to identify areas where we could do early, voluntary, sectoral liberalization using the model of the Information Technology Agreement. There were 62 proposals put forward during the summer; they have been consolidated to about 40. We are looking for a commercially significant package.

But U.S. leadership in this will only be able to lead if other economies look at us and know that we have the authority to carry out the proposals that we are making, so that, for instance, on energy goods and services, on environmental goods and services or on medical goods and services, three areas where the United States is a leading supplier, provider—those are areas that are prime-time attention for this early, voluntary, sectoral liberalization.

But what is Ambassador Barshefsky to say on the 21st of November when her colleagues say to her, these are good ideas but you are not going to have the authority to move forward on these, why should we agree to this? The same will be true in the WTO, whether it is for ITA–2 or whether it is for the building agenda that is coming.

There are important negotiations coming on agriculture, on services, on intellectual property rights, and all of those things are discussions that are under way now. The vote you take tomorrow is a vote for whether America will lead and whether we will compete, or whether we will retreat, and so I will stick with tomorrow.

Mr. BEREUTER. What do you think would be the particular criticisms to which the United States would be subjected in Vancouver by the other member States if, in fact, the Congress is not able, not successful, in an effort to approve fast track and grant the President and his trade negotiators those authorities?

Ambassador WOLF. If that happens, we will not be able to knock down the barriers that block Americans from providing goods and services into markets that are currently not as open as they should be. APEC is about building the marketplace and opening the marketplace. They go hand in hand. Our leadership is an imperative part of it. We will not be able to lead.

For the President, in 1993, he went to Blake Island in the wake of a successful vote on NAFTA and that enabled APEC leaders to give a strong boost to the completion of the Uruguay Round and that was important.

Last year, it was President Clinton and his hard work, with a number of leaders moving—some of the ones that you mentioned earlier, that moved forward the whole question of an Information Technology Agreement, that reduced to zero by the year 2000 tariffs on a wide range of information technology products. It was the President who had the power, and he had the authority, and he could provide the leadership that made that happen. $500 billion of trade has been liberalized as a result of that. That is the kind of leadership we are talking about.

After that $500 billion of liberalization in areas where we are the world leaders, we turned our attention to the global telecommunications service talks. Again, another $500 billion of global liberalization. Again, it is American companies that provide the hardware and the services in the international telecommunications field.

These are the kinds of things we can do when we have the authority and when we can lead. These are the kinds of things that are very hard to do when the people on the other side of the table say, you don't count because you can't deliver.

Mr. BEREUTER. Thank you for that response. I think it is very important to have that on the record.

I do want to ask you, what sectors have you designated as being open for negotiations without fast track approval and approval by Congress, since the Administration is using a sectoral free trade agreement as one way of attempting to achieve global free trade? What areas are open despite the importance of fast track authority?

Ambassador WOLF. I think we have a few residual pieces of fast track authority in areas like nonferrous metals and oil seeds and, I think, in forest products. These are several of the 40-plus areas that APEC is looking at; but frankly, in the areas that have won the widest support during the course of the summer and fall, areas like the environment, medical goods and services and energy goods and services, we do not have that authority. So that the ones where APEC is moving to some kind of a consensus, we hope—and it still requires a lot of work between now and the leaders' meeting—these are areas where we need the authority.

I think, in general, it is the whole question of whether we arrive with authority and looking to the next century to set the stage for the next century, or whether we arrive kind of on the last wisps of fuel in our tank. I think we do better to fill up our tank before we start this drive into the next century.

Mr. BEREUTER. Ambassador Wolf, what consideration has been given, if any, to ensuring that processed food is included as a priority sector for APEC trade liberalization?

Ambassador WOLF. There is a proposal that has been put out that includes processed food, and we would be delighted to support it.

Food is hard in APEC. It is one of the sensitive areas for several of the economies. The proposal that was first put forward by Australia has been going through a number of permutations. It still includes processed food, and we have been working closely with Australia on that one. But as I say, we are not going to get all of them this year in APEC.

We are looking for a commercially significant package, and I am not real good at handicapping the field, but I will tell you that food and some of the primary commodities are the hardest for some of the APEC economies, especially those in northeast Asia. I think the message that came to those economies' officials at the meeting in Singapore that we had 10 days ago was pretty clear. There are some important areas out there in the primary sectors. You are going to have to make a choice; you cannot choose none.

Mr. BEREUTER. I do think it is difficult, at times, in the agricultural sectors to make progress, but it seems to me, oftentimes in very specific areas, it is not as difficult to do it on processed food. In some cases, the resistance has no real competitive base in those economies. It is just thought—that is, related to agriculture—that it is too difficult. I do not think that always follows.

Ambassador WOLF. I think you are precisely right, Mr. Chairman. Some foreign ministries and trade ministries have a wedge theory which is that if you let them put the wedge in at all, the next thing you know, you will have everybody else coming through that door.

It is true, we are going to push those areas, and even as we push those areas in terms of broad liberalization, the tariff issues, there is work that we are doing in a number of sectors which are sensitive, that have to do with standards and testing and trying to decrease the transaction costs. So food is one area where we are working on phytosanitary standards. The automotive sector is another area where we think that there are things that are maybe too hard to do if you just say liberalization, but are easier to do if you say facilitation. But for us, for American workers and for American businesses, they can make a real dollars-and-cents difference in terms of our competitiveness. So those are specific areas on which we will also work.

Mr. BEREUTER. The example I always like to bring up is the subject of soup. I bring it up with respect to Taiwan. Taiwan has no soup companies, but you would not know it by looking at their tariff schedule. Taiwanese consume huge amounts of soup. So I bring that up even though the soup companies in my district are not likely to be beneficiaries in a direct sense of those plans. It is an example that I use occasionally.

Ambassador WOLF. I think they still prefer mother's soup or something.

Mr. BEREUTER. Well, some of them do. But they do not always have time over lunch to go home to mother.

[Laughter.]

Finally I would ask you, Ambassador, to what extent do you think that there will be special consideration or issues raised that relate to the currency, the stock market problems in Southeast Asia on the one hand, and second, very differently, to what extent do you think that the haze problem in Southeast Asia will be a factor in any of the discussions in Vancouver?

Ambassador WOLF. I think both of those issues overshadow—no pun intended—but both of those issues are the issues which shape the whole discussion, and they have shaped the discussion for the last several months. They will clearly be major issues at the ministerial and at the leaders' meeting on the financial and currencies volatility. Those are clearly issues to be discussed. At the root of the volatility—and I have several professionals sitting right behind me—I do not want to go too far.

But our sense is that sound macroeconomic policies and wise use of limited capital is an important prescription for reducing the likelihood of further swings now and future swings. So the discussion that finance officials are having in the APEC area is about how we can do things together to cooperate and coordinate, and how we can reduce, how we can get those sound, wise financial policies and mechanisms in place.

On the haze issue, this is sort of twofold. One issue is the haze issue in Southeast Asia, and there we are looking at ways in which the United States can build on some of the work that we have been doing with Indonesia over the last few weeks. We have three C–130's and a number of experts in forest fire management in Indonesia. There are things that we are going to look at in terms of weather prediction, institution building to deal with El Nino and vice versa. There are also things that we are going to look at, Canadians are interested in looking at as well, and other countries, in terms of emergency preparedness. That is one set of issues on the environment.

The second set of issues will not have an APEC conclusion, I am sure, but there will certainly be a discussion of the question of global climate change. I think what the haze makes clear is that the threats to our environment, the carbon-based gases and whatnot, are not just coming from developed countries. It is a problem that everybody shares in, and it is a solution that everyone must participate in jointly. I am certain that whether in the formal plenaries or at the retreats, and certainly in the bilaterals that we, the Japanese and others will be having very active discussions with the members of APEC on this critical issue for the next century.

Mr. BEREUTER. Thank you, Ambassador. I would hope that we might have your cooperation in responding to any questions that you might receive in writing from Members of the Subcommittee. I particularly want to extend that to the Minority since they are not able to be here at this point, but to all Members; is that possible?

Ambassador WOLF. We will be delighted. I hope you recognize that we are just 5 days away from this meeting of 36 ministers, 18 leaders and 1,400 of their closest friends just from the United States. We will do that.

Mr. BEREUTER. I do not think you can expect to receive any questions from Members within the next 2 days, in any case.

Ambassador WOLF. Then we will handle it in a very timely way.

Mr. BEREUTER. Our timing may be mutually agreeable here.

Ambassador WOLF. Thank you, Mr. Chairman. We would be delighted. You have been a strong supporter of open trade and opening the marketplace. You have been a strong supporter of the efforts that we make, and we thank you for that and for the voice that you take onto the House floor. I can't overstate how important these kinds of issues are.

I was in Savannah, Georgia, yesterday and I have done a lot of traveling around the United States, both in this job and as ambassador to Malaysia. When I go to American companies and I see American workers on the job because of the things that we are able to do, that comes in large part because we have been able to lead. We provide a credible leadership in trade and finance. Those people are at work and they are on Main Street spending money because of the involvement in the international global economy.

Some people can argue about whether it is good or bad to have a global economy. It exists and there is not really any going back. That is why your vote tomorrow is a critical vote. It is a vote that says we are going to go forward and we are going to stay at the front. We thank you for your help on that.

Mr. BEREUTER. Thank you, Ambassador. I have been intrigued with the view that we see expressed here, the view that people would like to stop the world. They don't like the way the world is headed. "Stop the world, I want to get off."

The alternative of NAFTA was to export even more jobs, and in fact, we eliminated some of the incentives for moving American jobs to Mexico by the passage of NAFTA. But not everybody looks at it that way. They simply did not like the direction, so they strike out and vote no without any real rational basis for that kind of decision.

Ambassador WOLF. I think Charlene Barshefsky made an interesting statement when she said that 80 percent of the job losses that have taken place in the American economy have been job losses due to productivity gain and technology. They are not due to trade.

These things are going to happen. That is why we have a sound economy. That is why we have lower unemployment and low inflation and that is one of the things that helped us get almost to a balanced budget.

Mr. BEREUTER. Thank you very much, Ambassador Wolf.

I will now call the second panel. I have introduced the members of the panel with a short biographical statement. Apparently Senator Johnston is not here yet.

I would like, first, to call upon Mr. Robert Denham, chairman of Salomon Inc., member of the APEC Business Advisory Council. Thank you very much for your effort to come here, for the testimony you are about to deliver and for your responses to questions later. Your entire statement will be made a part of the record. You may proceed as you wish.

STATEMENT OF ROBERT DENHAM, CHAIRMAN, SALOMON INC., AND MEMBER, APEC BUSINESS ADVISORY COUNCIL

Mr. DENHAM. Thank you, Mr. Chairman. I very much appreciate the opportunity to discuss with you the issues that will be raised, the recommendations that will be made at the Fifth Summit of the Asia Pacific Economic Cooperation Forum in Vancouver later this month.

APEC plays an important role in furthering trade and investment among the countries in the Asia Pacific region. In the present circumstances of market turmoil, APEC can encourage greater stability through policy coordination, through restoration of investment flows.

In 1996, I was appointed by President Clinton to the APEC Business Advisory Council, ABAC. ABAC is composed of senior business leaders from each of the 18 Asia Pacific economies reporting to the economic leaders. Like most of the business leaders participating in ABAC, my company, Salomon, benefits greatly from economic liberalization and enhanced trade as new opportunities are created for us and for our clients.

The APEC economic ministers asked for the creation of ABAC to advise and make recommendations to the leaders regarding challenges facing them. ABAC members have supported the adoption of policies which would advance freer and more stable flows of capital, facilitate private sector participation in infrastructure development and promote the development of financial and capital markets. The goals of ABAC are also the goals of U.S. workers, businesses and consumers: to enhance economic growth by creating broader and more efficient markets for goods, services and capital. The U.S. ABAC representatives have the additional goal of ensuring that U.S. companies and U.S. workers obtain maximum benefit from the rapid growth of APEC markets.

Last year, ABAC made recommendations to the APEC leaders in Manila. These recommendations addressed barriers to foreign direct investment, the financing of infrastructure projects, and recommended specific measures to increase the pace of trade liberalization and enhance business mobility. Our recommendations this year are meant to advance last year's program while improving upon and sharpening the focus.

I will give a few highlights of this year's ABAC report. The first is our assessment of the Manila Action Plan for APEC, or MAPA, which the 18 governments released last year in November, and our suggestions for improving action plans in the future. The second area contains our recommendations to the economic leaders in the areas of cross-border flows, financial and investment issues and economic and technical cooperation.

Regarding ABAC's assessment of the Manila Action Plan, ABAC is well aware that APEC plans continuously to update and improve its action plans in the coming years. We welcome this intention, and in assessing MAPA our primary goal has been offering recommendations for improving future action plans. These action plans constitute the essential link between APEC's grand vision of trade liberalization and the implementation by individual members that so crucially affects business.

From a business perspective, we found that the individual action plans compiled in MAPA are quite vague, generally nontransparent, lacking in specifics about the actions that member economies plan to take to reach the goal of free trade and investment by 2010 or 2020. APEC members need to be more specific about tariff and nontariff barriers. The action plans fail to offer additional commitments with regard to tariff and nontariff barriers beyond what members have already promised in the WTO or other multilateral organizations.

With respect to services, ABAC is encouraging APEC to take a leading role in bringing the WTO financial services talks to a successful conclusion this year and, in the medium term, take a comprehensive approach to removing impediments across the full range of service industries. In the critical area of foreign direct investment ABAC found little in MAPA by way of specific commitments to remove barriers.

In general, while APEC in the MAPA process produced fine-sounding principles or descriptions of best practices, these nonbinding collective principles are not being translated into concrete action by individual members.

In terms of our recommendations to leaders this year, ABAC will recommend that the leaders endorse the adoption of steps that will help capital markets facilitate economic growth. Specifically, we have put forth recommendations addressing currency instability, promoting regulation and transparency in financial markets, establishing modern clearance and settlement systems, developing understandable and harmonized accounting standards, broadening the local investor base and liberalizing foreign access. We urge the economic leaders to endorse public-private sector cooperation to facilitate development of markets for asset-backed securities in the region.

Additionally, in the area of cross-border flows, our report offers specific proposals to facilitate business travel, improve enforcement of intellectual property rights, harmonize standards for business-related professional services and establish more open and competitive government procurement systems. These recommendations are aimed at reducing the cost of cross-border business in the APEC region.

The report also expresses support for APEC efforts to identify sectors for early voluntary liberalization. Some examples of sectors where ABAC believes early action might occur include chemicals, environmental projects and services, food, oil seeds, pharmaceuticals, pulp and wood products, toys, automotive and other transport products. In the area of finance, investment and infrastructure, our recommendations are aimed at promoting more private investment in infrastructure, at developing the region's capital markets, and at easing financing for small- and medium-sized companies and developing tax treaties to eliminate double taxation of firms that operate in more than one APEC economy.

The region's critical infrastructure needs can only be met if we enhance private investment in large-scale infrastructure projects in the region. For APEC to respond effectively to this need, we recommend a sectoral approach to investment liberalization for infrastructure through an infrastructure investment initiative. This initiative applies enhanced investment protection on a sectoral basis to infrastructure projects. It builds on our APEC voluntary investment project, known as AVIP, which calls for APEC to encourage a strong system of investment protection measures on a project-by-project basis. Under this initiative, APEC economies would be encouraged to apply a strong regime of investment protection meas-

47-149 - 98 - 2

ures to the infrastructure sector generally in order to attract more private investment.

Recent market instability is a very serious issue that is of high concern to ABAC members. Business needs a predictable macroeconomic environment, including stable foreign exchange markets. Relatively free flowing international capital has been a key ingredient in the region's economic success. Such openness, however, places an extra premium on sound macroeconomic management by economies. ABAC hopes that APEC economies will cooperate on this issue, which should include developing transparent and timely national economic statistics to provide early warning of macroeconomic imbalances. It should also include collective review of members' macroeconomic policies, should include developing and enforcing rules against market manipulation, and developing and administering appropriate adjustment funds in cooperation with the IMF and, finally, and importantly, should include continuing financial sector liberalization.

For the United States to continue to play a leadership role in groupings such as APEC, it is essential that we get a renewal of fast track trade negotiating authority. Trade liberalization and a stable investment environment benefits U.S. workers and U.S. businesses and creates markets for U.S. exports. Through new trade negotiations, the United States will continue to lead the APEC economies toward further trade liberalizing policies, with the elimination of some of the same trade and financial access barriers that are being discussed today. Without fast track authority, U.S. leadership on trade and a broad range of other important national economic issues would be impossible.

I think it is important to recognize that the vote on fast track is being taken at a time of substantial turmoil in the world's financial markets. As one observes financial markets over a long period of time, one of the conclusions you come to is that financial markets are influenced powerfully by changes in direction in economic policy. If fast track were to be denied, I think this would be viewed as a significant change in the direction of U.S. economic policy in the postwar period. The consequences of that to financial markets in the long run and perhaps even the short run might be serious.

As a member of ABAC, I look forward to the opportunity to exchange views with the APEC leaders in Vancouver just as I have appreciated this opportunity to present my views to your Subcommittee. Thank you, Mr. Chairman.

[The prepared statement of Mr. Denham appears in the appendix.]

Mr. BEREUTER. Mr. Denham, thank you very much.

Your testimony deserves very careful scrutiny. I do hope that you have the attention of the APEC meeting when you make these recommendations on the capital market, its role in facilitating economic growth and suggested changes you have on the elements of the macroeconomic policy that affect the environment there. You certainly should have, in light of what has happened lately.

Senator Johnston, welcome. Glad to see you here. Nice to have you back in the halls of the Congress. I introduced you previously as having long demonstrated a strong and very knowledgeable interest in the Asia Pacific region and in trade generally. That is absolutely true. We appreciate very much your contribution and the fact that you have taken time to be with us today.

I am faced with a vote and, before we begin, in order that your presentation and that of Fred Bergsten is not interrupted, I would like to take a 10-minute recess. I think I can complete the vote and be back with you. The Subcommittee will be in recess for 10 minutes.

[Recess.]

Mr. BEREUTER. The Subcommittee will come to order. Our next witness is The Honorable Bennett Johnston. Senator, you may proceed as you wish.

STATEMENT OF THE HONORABLE J. BENNETT JOHNSTON, FORMER MEMBER OF UNITED STATES SENATE FROM THE STATE OF LOUISIANA, PRESIDENT, U.S.-PECC, PACIFIC ECONOMIC COOPERATION COUNCIL

Senator JOHNSTON. Thank you very much, Mr. Chairman. This is my first trip back up here since I retired in January. It is nice to be back. I am testifying on behalf of Pacific Economic Cooperation Council (PECC). I am president of what we call U.S.-PECC. I have a formal written statement, Mr. Chairman, but I would like to proceed in a briefer style if I may.

Mr. BEREUTER. That is certainly appropriate. Your entire statement will be made a part of the record.

Senator JOHNSTON. Mr. Chairman, there has been a tremendous evolution about our collective thinking about Asia. We used to think of Asia as being just lots of people, lots of poverty and lots of problems. Now we think of it as huge prosperity and opportunity, but still problems. This year, of course, has been very extraordinary and historic: Hong Kong, new security relationship with Japan, famine in Korea, and of course more recently the terrible financial crises in Southeast Asia, the full extent of which we do not know yet. What we do realize is how deeply and directly Asia affects America, its future and its security as well as its economy.

In 1980, the Prime Ministers of Australia and Japan recognized that there was a need for a forum to which members of the Pacific community could go for common discussions and to deal with problems. They called a conference which was attended by 12 countries and set up PECC. It was founded as a tripartite group, business, government as well as academics. For the first few years, they conducted research, educated the members, and advocated the need for a group like APEC. By 1989, the first APEC conference was called. It was meant to be a one of a kind but it now has a permanent charter, if not a permanent standing in the laws of the various countries.

APEC is the only forum for the common discussion of economic policy debates and initiatives in Asia. It is vitally important. As you know, there are APEC summit meetings as well as ministerial meetings attended by our Secretary of State, our Trade Representative and Secretary of Commerce.

The method of APEC, and I know I am being very fundamental, is rather difficult to assess in some people's eyes in that it relies on individual commitments as opposed to treaties. It is a very delicate process to have all of these countries jointly declare their individual commitments to various trade and economic policies as opposed to having a binding agreement. Sometimes the commitments are in very broad terms, as the Bogor, Indonesia commitment to open economies in Asia by the year 2010.

PECC plays a very important role, not only in initially setting it up but also being its advocate. PECC identifies, researches and tees up the issues for APEC. One of the biggest projects we have done at the behest of APEC is a survey of the impediments to trade and investment in the whole region. Additional work has now been agreed to and will be undertaken by PECC. Another example is telecommunications, where we are dealing with removing impediments to trade, seeking common standards, terminal testing, certification, et cetera. As you can imagine, in international trade and telecommunications, it is vitally important that our equipment match, that we know what the fields of competition are and how we define our common standards and how we remove the impediments for American businesses to get into not only telecommunications but other areas.

We are dealing with items like intellectual property, which is a huge area of concern to American companies, legal liability, rule of law, content issues, et cetera. We are organized into 10 working groups, telecommunications, energy, finance, transport, fisheries, human resources, minerals, trade policy, food and agriculture, and an economic forecasting group led by Professor Lawrence Krause.

PECC research narrows the areas for negotiation. We identify issues for APEC and help solve them. As such, PECC is the only business and government network for research that exists in all APEC economies. There are about 100 council members in the United States. Internationally, PECC is virtually all volunteers, with some officers principally paid by their respective governments. Many of the researchers are from academe and receive only travel expenses.

I talk about this because, frankly, we need your help. Each year, the United States is supposed to pay $72,000 to fund the Secretariat in Singapore and assist some travel by scholars. The vast bulk of what we do is funded by business and by individual volunteers. I am embarrassed to tell you, Mr. Chairman, that the United States is in arrears to this organization to the tune of about $320,000, a drop in the bucket, not even enough to talk about in the great halls of Congress. But as president of U.S.-PECC, I attend these meetings and they believe I am going to come in and say, well, of course, we have solved the problem. At a recent meeting down in Santiago, I arrived a few minutes late and Adlai Stevenson, our former U.S.-PECC president, filled in for me. They had asked him about the funding and he said, do not worry, Senator Johnston will be here to talk about how he has solved this problem.

Mr. BEREUTER. It is nice to be put on the spot. Congressman Richardson, now our ambassador, has the same problem in the United Nations. It is a little larger scale.

Senator JOHNSTON. I know. But he has got some people's attention. We do not yet. So we need your help to make some people aware. Also the State Department feels that it would come out of its budget and so there is that concern.

Let me reiterate what the first speaker, Mr. Denham, said about fast track. We are predictably and very strongly for fast track. It is essential for the whole Asia Pacific region if we are to keep our influence and our credibility. We strongly support that.

Thank you very much for the opportunity to be here and for what I know will be your strong support of U.S.-PECC.

[The prepared statement of Senator Johnston appears in the appendix.]

Mr. BEREUTER. Thank you very much, Senator Johnston.

Now we will hear our third witness on the second panel, Dr. C. Fred Bergsten, director of the Institute for International Economics. I think this may be your third appearance before the Subcommittee since I have had a chance to chair it. Welcome back and thank you for your time and your efforts. We look forward to your testimony. Your entire statement will be part of the record. You may proceed.

STATEMENT OF DR. C. FRED BERGSTEN, DIRECTOR, INSTITUTE FOR INTERNATIONAL ECONOMICS

Dr. BERGSTEN. Mr. Chairman, thank you very much. It is a particular pleasure to be here this time, because, as you well know, my institute released a book just last month called *Wither APEC? The Progress to Date and Agenda for the Future.* I mention that because it has an extremely cogent and persuasive chapter written by the chairman of this Committee, Congressman Bereuter.

Mr. BEREUTER. Nice of you to mention that.

Dr. BERGSTEN. It is a very important part of our effort. I appreciated your involvement in our major conference on that topic last spring.

Looking to the upcoming APEC summit in Vancouver, trade issues have, of course, been and remain central to the APEC process. APEC, at its Bogor summit in 1994, enunciated the goal of achieving free trade and investment in the region by 2010 and 2020. If achieved, this will be the biggest trade agreement in history; countries that account for half the world's economy will have eliminated all of their barriers. The chosen instrument for liberalization now is sectoral agreements. APEC pushed the Information Technology Agreement through the WTO a year ago. There is still good reason to hope that APEC economies will be able to reach an agreement on financial services liberalization in Vancouver this year, which would in turn galvanize a WTO agreement on that sector in December.

Now, APEC is about to agree on a number of additional sectors—maybe four, five, or six additional sectors—for serious efforts to liberalize over the course of the next year. As Ambassador Wolf said, that agenda can proceed, and the United States can lead it, only with the passage of fast track. So I would add my voice to yours and to that of the other witnesses today in suggesting that the fast-track vote tomorrow is absolutely crucial for the future of APEC and U.S. market opportunities in the Asia Pacific region as well as many other regions.

I would furthermore underline what Mr. Denham said. If this House were to explicitly turn down fast track tomorrow, I believe there would be a devastating impact on the financial markets. The world economy has proceeded for 30 years on the assumption of international economic cooperation and active U.S. leadership in that process. A rejection of fast track would shatter that assumption.

I have tracked these relationships over the years. Whenever the Congress has taken even small steps toward restricting our markets or backing away from international cooperation, the dollar has dropped sharply in the exchange markets. That was even in calm times. In today's very nervous and fragile market conditions, I would have no hesitance in predicting that if you explicitly reject this on Friday, next Monday will be a very black Monday, and there will be a devastating effect not only on our financial markets but on financial markets around the world, because one of the critical assumptions of the whole basis for world economic progress would be thrown into question. So, that consideration must be in Members' minds when you vote tomorrow.

Mr. BEREUTER. Dr. Bergsten, that is a very sobering prediction. If in fact we take that action, I hope that everybody will note that and give it a special emphasis today, tomorrow in the media. You know we already rejected a Caribbean Basin initiative reform bill in the House unfortunately this week. So that would be a much harsher blow. Thank you, you may proceed. I am sorry to interrupt you.

Dr. BERGSTEN. Let me turn to the focus of my statement, which closely relates to these same market issues. In addition to the trade topics at Vancouver, I believe that the APEC summit should launch new arrangements to support and reinforce IMF in helping to prevent and respond to future monetary crises in the region. Indeed, I believe that Vancouver should be "the finance summit", which would add a major new dimension to APEC's agenda for dealing with Asia Pacific problems. There is a clear need for additional monetary arrangements. I believe a consensus is evolving to put such arrangements in place.

As Ambassador Wolf said, the Deputy Finance Ministers of the APEC countries, including the Deputy Secretary of our own Treasury, will be meeting to discuss these issues at Manila on November 18 and 19, trying to put concrete plans together. There is a consensus on a need for new arrangements, but as far as I can tell, there is no consensus at all at this point on where and how to do it. I would submit, Mr. Chairman, that APEC is the logical institutional home for the new Asian Monetary Fund that has been discussed so widely since the onset of the current financial problems in Southeast Asia.

Incidentally, the ideas that I put before you today are not only my own; they are supported by an independent panel of experts, a group that has been meeting regularly over the last several years to try to offer independent expert advice to the APEC governments on what policies they might pursue. I attach to my statement our latest report, which addresses these issues in some detail. I might add that the ideas I mention today strike me as being fully consistent with, though more detailed than, the suggestions from the APEC Business Advisory Council (ABAC) that Mr. Denham enunciated a few moments ago.

Ambassador Wolf is right; there is no silver bullet that APEC is going to adopt in Vancouver that will resolve the current monetary crisis or solve all our problems. The primary goal of what I recommend for APEC would be to prevent future crises, not serve as a bailout fund.

After the Mexican financial crisis in early 1995, there were extensive efforts to improve the early warning system. But the system failed again in Thailand, and one might add Indonesia. Moreover, the contagion to neighboring countries is far worse on this occasion than it was in Latin America in 1995.

I hasten to add that the IMF, as I see it, did its job in foreseeing and warning of the impending problem. The systemic difficulty was that Thailand rejected the advice, and no one pressed it to act. The IMF on its own demonstrably cannot get countries to adjust preemptively. The best prospect, in my view, is to get the neighboring countries to intervene or press for preventative action because they are so likely to be hurt themselves by the fallout from a crisis.

In the Asia Pacific region, I think APEC can provide the institutional locus for such efforts. It has already been developing an extensive process of peer pressure, or friendly persuasion, through which individual members encourage others to act responsibly and in the interest of the broadest group as well as in their own interest. APEC is using this approach to pursue its Bogor target of free trade in the region. The most dramatic success came at last year's Subic summit, when peer pressure did persuade a number of members to eliminate their tariffs on a wide range of high tech products, enabling APEC to galvanize the ITA on $500 billion worth of trade. I am sure, Mr. Chairman, that you have talked to President Clinton about this. He felt that APEC was enormously successful last year, because its process did convert the views of a number of countries, indicating that peer pressure can work.

In the monetary area, the APEC finance ministers have been meeting regularly since the Seattle summit. Their deputies have convened even more often and are doing so in Manila in 2 weeks. They have already discussed the currency and related issues in depth. I believe they should begin systematically assessing national economic outlooks, pressing members to adopt good advice from the IMF and elsewhere that would head off future crises and thereby avoid new disruption in the region.

In addition, though they could simply create this new surveillance mechanism, I think APEC should also create a standby funding arrangement to support future IMF programs in the region. The current cases are only the latest reminders that such crises inevitably occur from time to time and that international rescue packages will be required in the future as in the past. It is also clear that IMF lending by itself will never be adequate. The IMF has plenty of money. That is not the problem. The problem is that IMF credits to any individual country are limited by that country's quota in the IMF. Even when the IMF gives generous multiples of quotas—700 percent to Mexico, 500 percent to Thailand—it is still only a small part of the total package that is needed to reassure markets and get the country to take the corrective action.

Widespread support has therefore developed for a so-called Asian Monetary Fund to supplement the IMF. Japan proposed an Asia-only fund, but, for alot of reasons, it has been rejected, including by the proposed beneficiaries. China, incidentally, is totally opposed to it. ASEAN is obviously too small a group to create such a fund on its own.

So I conclude that APEC is the logical institutional venue. It includes all the Asian countries that might need help. It includes all the potential creditors, including the United States and Canada as well as Japan, Singapore, Hong Kong, China, Taiwan, and Brunei. Its Latin American members would be helpful, Mexico with its crisis and dramatic recovery experience and Chile as a healthy role model.

The main criticism of this proposal is that any standing fund would create a so-called moral hazard, raising the risk of profligate policies and unsound investments that would bring on a crisis rather than head it off. There is a decisive answer to that concern, which is simply to tie any APEC arrangements inextricably to IMF programs. No country is going to put itself through the ringer of a monetary crisis and subject itself to the tender mercies of the IMF simply because some rescue funds are available, nor would private investors keep coming when there are countless alternative opportunities around the world if the IMF requires them to share the cost of adjustment programs, as it must.

Since we are going to have programs of this type from time to time, the alternative to a standby arrangement is simply ad hoc bailouts, as cobbled together by the United States for Mexico and Japan for Thailand. Their outcome is always highly uncertain, as when the Congress almost blocked the Mexican package. Their magnitude, how donors share obligations, and speed of delivery are purely fortuitous. Prepared standby funding is far superior.

Therefore, in conclusion, Mr. Chairman, I believe that the APEC summit at Vancouver has an enormous opportunity. It can and should launch new preventive and funding arrangements to deal with future monetary crises in this region.

In 1993, APEC decided to create a community of Asia Pacific economies. The community now requires better mechanisms to avoid and handle future crises. In 1994, APEC decided to achieve free trade in the region. It now needs comparably bold initiatives on the financial side. In 1996, APEC effectively applied peer pressure to achieve the Information Technology Agreement. It now needs to use similar techniques to head off monetary disruptions.

Vancouver can be "the finance summit" that will add to this chain of dramatic successes and further mark APEC as the outstanding international institutional innovation of the post-cold war era.

Thank you very much.

[The prepared statement of Dr. Bergsten appears in the appendix.]

Mr. BEREUTER. Thank you very much, Dr. Bergsten, for your stimulating presentation.

I would like to begin with nearly the last point that Dr. Bergsten brought up—that is, his proposal to create a standby funding arrangement to support further IMF programs in the area. This has not, of course, been on the previous U.S. agenda—perhaps unprecedented. You have heard, I think completely, the materials that he has in his formal presentation, his arguments for it and the tie to the IMF programs. I would like the other two witnesses, if they have any comments, to comment upon it. Would you like to be first?

Mr. DENHAM. Mr. Chairman, I think that there are many interesting aspects of Dr. Bergsten's proposal. It is worthy of serious attention. In my mind one of the most important issues is the relationship of any such fund to the IMF because I think it is very important that the IMF have primacy and centrality to the process of working out the adjustment programs. The IMF has demonstrated the ability to work out adjustment programs, develop adjustment programs, the ability to work with countries to get countries to go along with its programs and the will to stick with those programs. That last point is important, having the will to stick with the insistence on tough medicine.

I think there is a danger that an Asian fund, certainly if it got decoupled from the IMF process, would not have that necessary will. It is a little like if I get behind on my car payments, the bank is not going to put my brother-in-law in charge of my finances, and we do not want to have that sort of process existing as an Asian currency fund. I am sure that is not at all what Dr. Bergsten has in mind. But I do think the question of centrality of the IMF is critical.

I also welcome Dr. Bergsten's emphasis on the prevention of future crises, and his point about the situation in Thailand is important. This was identified by the IMF. It was identified by a number of people. But it was not possible to get the necessary attention by the Thai government.

I think there is a very important role for APEC to play, the APEC finance ministers to play, in talking with each other to focus the attention of countries that are developing imbalances in their macroeconomic conditions, get another country to focus on the problem that they are heading toward. I think that that is something we should be encouraging APEC to do.

Senator JOHNSTON. Mr. Chairman, there is, as you know, a great competition for the hearts and minds of people in Asia as to first assigning fault for what the present problems are and, second, prescribing the medicine. On the one hand, Prime Minister Mahathir, who spoke at our PECC conference down in Santiago, would assign that fault to Western speculators and Westerners who want to take advantage of these emerging companies. He states that basically nothing is wrong, nothing needs correcting other than to deal with controlling the outside speculators.

My own belief is that in each of these countries, Indonesia, Thailand, all of them that have problems, most of which have bubbled to the surface and some of which perhaps have yet to appear, all have been caused by identifiable and clear problems which were preventable. We cannot repeal altogether the economic cycle anywhere, particularly not in Southeast Asia. The solutions involve the countries doing things that they do not want to do. I could go right down the list. In Indonesia some of these things were just announced. They closed some of the banks, and that is causing a great debate. The national car company may be moved. The same set of tough medicines are proposed elsewhere and may or may not be carried out.

Now, the question is not whether they need help and the terms of a fund. I think that there needs to be a fund. The question is how well can we fashion a delivery mechanism that makes them accept the discipline.

My own view is that the IMF, in coordination with APEC or APEC in coordination with IMF, as Fred Bergsten says, can be made to be a very effective instrument. The Asian way seems to be to do things by consensus and the APEC way is to do things by consensus. IMF, on the other hand, tends to be authoritarian. They issue the orders and you have to agree with them.

So I think a proper melding of the two, where you have the appearance of consensus through APEC but the delivery mechanism through the IMF that enforces these disciplines is the way to do it. That is only stating things in a very broad way. The difficulty comes in the details. I personally, and I am speaking now personally because PECC has not taken a position on this, believe that the Vancouver summit offers a very good place to begin discussions as to how we fashion a mechanism to deliver help but also deliver the discipline.

Mr. BEREUTER. Thank you, Senator. Thank you, Mr. Denham.

Dr. Bergsten, I am going to ask you to comment in a minute on the recommendations in the Denham paper, which are not his own but which are from the organization he represents: on page 4, his recommendations about the ways to help capital market facilitate economic growth and then the elements to give a more predictable macroeconomic environment on page 5. If you could just scan those briefly. I will shift to Senator Johnston in the meantime.

Senator, if we looked at what Congress can do better to advance the important priorities and objectives of APEC—which generally I think we understand and certainly will benefit the United States, as most of us see it—one of the immediate issues is fast track. We have had some discussion about that. I agree with the importance of doing that. Beyond that, certainly, there is an educational function that we have. I have been trying in a small way to do that. I recall a couple years ago when I would mention APEC in the elevator or something like that, just dropping that name there in the midst of a conversation, and people would confuse it with OPIC and AIPAC, and, "What is this APEC?" So that is one of the reasons why we have had at least 3, maybe 4 years in the last several years. That is an education function we have to pursue. What else can you think of now, looking back, not from a very long distance? What in the Senate, what in the House could we do to advance the objectives of APEC and trade liberalization that we pursue through that organization?

Senator JOHNSTON. Mr. Chairman, I think you have identified the problems. The problem is that in the Congress so few people know anything about Asia. They don't know what APEC is, they certainly don't know what U.S.-PECC is, and they don't know what these problems are. Too many Members of Congress react to pressure groups, whether or not they be for great goals. They tend to look at a trade problem as if it is a problem of one-dimensional human rights or one-dimensional religious liberty or native rights or the environment without understanding the complexities of these emerging economies. And they are very, very complex. The history, the development of each of these countries in Southeast Asia is very complicated. It cannot be simplified. We cannot control it by reacting in an emotional way to the pressure groups.

I say that because these actions are proliferating. I think there are some 70 different sanctions that our government has taken against countries, and I do not know of any of them that have really worked. Some have been counterproductive. They take the place of real policy. This is not to say that these issues, from the environment to human rights and all the rest, do not have a very great place and an important place, but we need to react with knowledge rather than just visceral responses to the pressure of groups. For that reason, one of the most important things that can be done is to get Members to go to Asia. I went to Indonesia, I think it was about 4 years ago. It was the first visit by any Member of Congress in a year and a half. It is a long way over there. But people need to understand about this huge country, the largest Moslem country in the world, with over 200 million people. This applies to all Asia. It is far away, but it is very important to everything we do in this country.

Mr. BEREUTER. Thank you. Do you know there is a Trans-Atlantic Business Council where you have legislators and now business people from both sides of the Atlantic involved in a more routine process? I wonder, is there anything that lends itself to a greater flow of information between APEC and the United States? Does PECC? Do you have some way of getting more information about what you do and are trying to accomplish to Members of Congress as well as to the executive branch? I think you are sending your information automatically to the executive branch or trying to get this to the Heads of State and the ministers that make the decisions; your recommendations surely will come to their attention as well as your foreign counterparts. Is there some way that you could contribute to a better understanding up here of what your objectives are? For example, if there is merit in some idea related to facilitating travel of businessmen in the APEC region by reducing visa requirements, is that something that you are having any success in advancing here as an idea?

Mr. DENHAM. I think the suggestion implicit in what you are saying, that we need to as the U.S. representatives to ABAC do a better job of communicating to Congress, is a very good suggestion and one that I have received and will make sure that we start doing a better job of that. I think there are a number of things, such as you just pointed out, on removing impediments to business travel that are extremely important to American businesses operating in Asia.

Interestingly enough, I think they are most important to small- and medium-size enterprises. A large company like mine has a lot of ways frequently to deal with issues of needing to move employees around. We have got a lot of alternatives. If one employee has a visa problem from the United States, maybe we can send someone from Japan or someone from Australia, a nation with a different passport. She is not going to have the same visa problem.

But a small- or medium-size enterprise does not have that kind of flexibility. That is a really biting issue for them.

I think that kind of issue would resonate with many people in Congress. We need to get those kinds of recommendations in front of them.

Mr. BEREUTER. This Trans-Atlantic Business Council—I am not forgetting what ocean we are talking about here—this dialog that has been taking place now embraced by the president of EU and President Clinton recently... Do you think there is any kind of potential parallel for the Asia Pacific region?

Mr. DENHAM. I think there may be. Of course there are groups like PECC and ABAC that provide a forum for business to communicate, but does not include the same kind of legislative involvement.

Mr. BEREUTER. We do not sit down with meetings where you explain why this is important as we are now trying to do with respect to the European Parliament Members and Members of Congress, with businessmen from Europe and America.

Mr. DENHAM. I think it could be very valuable to develop a forum for legislative involvement by legislators throughout the APEC region with businesses to talk about the kinds of things that come out of PECC and ABAC studies.

Senator JOHNSTON. Mr. Chairman, I think you are really onto something. One of the problems, however, is that so many of the countries in Asia do not have the traditional kinds of parliament with the same power as they do in Europe. So perhaps we should identify in those countries ministers at a comparable level of power just so that the government leaders, whoever they may be, would come and visit with us. I think it would be very, very helpful.

Mr. BEREUTER. That is a point well taken.

I know Mr. Denham has to leave. I want to have as a last element here, while all three of you are together, anything Dr. Bergsten would like to say about the suggestions of ABAC that I particularly identified for you. Would you like to make any comments?

Dr. BERGSTEN. Very quickly, I strongly support the ABAC proposals as Mr. Denham put them forward today. I think, particularly, that the changes to further strengthen the financial markets and to provide a stronger basis for financing the infrastructure needs of the region, which are huge, are terribly important. I very much like his stress on the sectoral approach, including within the infrastructure context.

I think ABAC has come up with a very creative idea, the so-called APEC Voluntary Investment Projects (AVIP). I always felt that if you could get APEC countries to instill investment protection on a case-by-case basis like that, it would then multiply like wildfire for competitive reasons. Once a given country does it for a given sector, then other countries will have to emulate. Once you get it implanted, it will spread and multiply. I think it is a very creative idea, and I strongly support it.

I also support his points on the macroeconomic environment. That is what I had in mind when I suggested that my proposals were consistent with those of the ABAC. In ticking off the ABAC proposals, he talked about a collective review of members' macroeconomic policies. That is what I had in mind with this new facility, to try to prevent crises and provide appropriate adjustment funds in cooperation with the IMF. I think these are very creative and very positive ideas.

I very much welcome both Mr. Denham's and Senator Johnston's support for my proposals. I would also like to echo their comment that you are really onto something with your idea of parliamentary exchanges. I have been involved in that on the Atlantic side. I think it would be very helpful on the Pacific side, partly to have routine involvement by our own Congressmen, which I know is one of your purposes. Also, to pick up on Senator Johnston's points, it is true that the other countries do not all have a parliament like we do, but maybe we could encourage them to move at least a bit in our direction by engaging them on a regular basis with our own parliamentarians. I think there would be a lot of benefits. I hope we will pursue this idea.

Mr. BEREUTER. Thank you very much.

There is this infant organization that has been evolving over there. Senator Roth has been heavily involved in it, among other of our Senate colleagues, I think.

Gentlemen, I want to thank you very much for your contributions here today. The interaction among you, I think, has been particularly helpful—to this Member at least. I very much appreciate your time. I know all of you are very busy. Dr. Bergsten, I think you, in particular, have a lot of people in the city right now that you are trying to host.

I will look forward to watching the Vancouver summit with even more interest than usual and would like to see how it really works sometime.

Thank you very much. I appreciate your coming.

This Subcommittee hearing is adjourned.

[Whereupon, at 3:35 p.m., the Subcommittee was adjourned.]

APPENDIX

STATEMENT BY AMBASSADOR JOHN S. WOLF
U.S. COORDINATOR FOR APEC

HOUSE INTERNATIONAL RELATIONS COMMITTEE
SUBCOMMITTEE ON EAST ASIA AND THE PACIFIC

NOVEMBER 6, 1997

"THE UNITED STATES AND APEC 1997"

Mr. Chairman, Distinguished Members:

I would like to thank the Committee for inviting me here today.

Some would say "Why discuss APEC now when the hot issues in the region and even globally appear to be finance and currency and not economic cooperation?" Why, because we care about the stability of the Asia- Pacific. We care because millions of Americans are of Asian and Pacific descent; because thousands of U.S. companies are involved in the region and because millions of American jobs depend on Asia's well being.

In his first term, President Clinton set forth a vision of a Pacific community based on a mutually reinforcing framework of "shared strength, shared prosperity and shared commitment to democratic values." APEC is the premiere multilateral economic forum for advancing those policies.

Up to this point, APEC's efforts have worked on two sides of the same issue: building the marketplace of the Asia-Pacific while at the same time ensuring that marketplace remains open.

That, incidently, is why tomorrow's vote on Fast Track is so important. This vote is about the ability of US firms to compete abroad, and it is about America's ability to continue the leadership which, ~~for over fifty years,~~ we have provide to the global trade and financial system . Events of these past few weeks make clear our economic interests are intertwined with Asia. We need to ~~have~~ the flexibility and the authority to continue the leadership we have exercised for over fifty years. What we must ask ourselves on fast track is: Are we going to make the rules, or sit back and let those who don't share our interests make them for us?

This year, APEC Leaders in Vancouver will have confront today's immediate issues -- issues related to how the region's economies can adjust to their recent economic difficulties, pursue necessary reform, and get back on the path to strong, sustainable economic growth.

Road to Vancouver

The United States is pursuing six issue/goals in the run-up to the APEC Leaders' Meeting in Vancouver:

First, we expect the Southeast Asia financial situation to be at the top top of many Leaders'. We've been making extraordinary efforts to help the countries of the region address the complex economic issues we all are reading about daily. U.S. involvement in support of the IMF program for Indonesia is a visible sign of that interest.

Finance officials in the APEC region are looking at how APEC can help promote and/or restore financial stability in Southeast Asia. But no one should imagine there will be some "silver bullet" that comes from the November Leaders' Meeting to solve all the region's problems. Improvement requires a steadfast commitment to sound policies and demonstrated efforts to adjust.

Second, APEC is in the process of identifying sectors for Early Voluntary Sectoral Liberalization. We want an outcome that is economically significant and one that help increase the attractiveness of projects in Asia -- infrastructure-related goods and services, for instance, fit this specification.

47-149 - 98 - 3

Third, we want to use APEC to clear the trade underbrush. New air express techniques to speed goods to customers and a Mutual Recognition Agreement (MRA) to eliminate needless retesting of telecommunications equipment are two examples.

APEC is not a traditional trade organization; we do not sit in mind-numbing negotiations. Our work is aimed at focused outcomes that increase economic efficiency, increase economic activity and assure more and better jobs, safer workplaces, and a cleaner environment. For this work, APEC can't depend just on government officials; there must be active private sector involvement.

Much of our work is focused on APEC's economic and technical cooperation (EcoTech) side. If APEC builds the right architecture for economic cooperation, businesses will be able to take advantage of the opportunities trade and investment liberalization create.

As a fourth goal for Vancouver, we would like to use APEC to build support for President Clinton's Electronic Commerce initiative.

This technology is new, but it is not a threat. It is the enabling technology of the next century. It's an area where APEC economies have a great deal to gain through encouraging the private sector to develop the infrastructure and the applications.

We believe that governments should intervene only minimally to create a stable environment for electronic commerce.

Fifth is an issue right out of today's headlines: climate change and the environment. The environmental issues are threats which demand our joint attention, our joint commitment and our joint action.

Finally, each APEC member economy has put forward an Individual Action Plan (IAP). These remain the essential road map of economies path to free trade and investment by 2010/2020.

The establishment of regional institutions such as APEC and the ASEAN Regional Forum are the first steps toward the building of a Pacific community that will solve its problems ***as a community***.

Ultimately, it is the soundness of this community, the commitment of its members to make it work and to share in the security, prosperity and values it has to offer, that will keep the economic dynamism of the Asia-Pacific region alive and expand it for all the world to share.

The Pacific community is real. And the United States will continue to be a vital part of it.

Thank you.

Drafted:	EAP/EP:RFHolden 647-4886
11/06/97 12:48 PM	o:/ep/apecpub/wolfhirc.doc
Approved:	EAP/EP:JAndre (ok)
Cleared:	EAP:JWolf (ok)
	EAP/FO:PYun (ok)
	EAP/PA:KBailes (ok)
	EAP/RSP:DKeegan (ok)
	E:SVillarosa (ok)
	PA/S:HHurlburt (ok)
	H:/DPittman (ok)

SALOMON INC

STATEMENT OF ROBERT E. DENHAM
CHAIRMAN AND CEO OF SALOMON INC
Before the
Subcommittee on Asia and the Pacific
The House Committee on International Relations
November 6, 1997

Thank you, Mr. Chairman and Members of the Committee. It is a pleasure to appear before you today. I am honored and very much appreciate the opportunity to discuss the financial infrastructure issues to be raised and recommendations to be made at the Fifth Summit of the Asia Pacific Economic Cooperation Forum in Vancouver, British Columbia later this month. The purpose of APEC forums has been to further political and economic ties among nations with disparate political systems and at different stages of development.

APEC plays an important role in furthering trade and investment among the countries in the Asia Pacific region. In the present circumstances of market turmoil, APEC can encourage greater stability through policy coordination and the restoration of investment flows.

In 1996, President Clinton appointed me to the APEC Business Advisory Council (ABAC). ABAC is comprised of senior business leaders from the APEC economies reporting to the Asia-Pacific Economic Cooperation forum. Like most of the business leaders participating in ABAC, my company, which is Salomon Inc, benefits greatly from economic liberalization and enhanced trade as new opportunities are created for ourselves and our clients.

The APEC economic ministers asked for the creation of ABAC in 1995 to advise and make recommendations to the Leaders of the APEC economies regarding challenges facing them. ABAC members have supported the adoption of policies which would advance freer and more stable flows of capital; facilitate private sector participation in infrastructure development; and promote the

SALOMON INC

development of financial and capital markets. The goals of ABAC are also the goals of U.S. workers, businesses and consumers – to enhance economic growth by creating broader and more efficient markets for goods, services and capital. The U.S. ABAC representatives have the additional goal of insuring that U.S. companies and workers can obtain maximum benefit from the rapid growth of APEC markets.

Last year, ABAC made recommendations to the APEC Leaders in Manila. These recommendations specifically addressed barriers to foreign direct investment and to the financing of infrastructure projects, and recommended specific measures to increase the pace of trade liberalization and enhance business mobility. ABAC's recommendations this year are meant to advance last year's recommendations, while improving upon and sharpening their focus.

I will give a few highlights of this year's Report, which consists of two main parts. The first is ABAC's assessment of the Manila Action Plan for APEC, or MAPA, which the 18 governments released in November 1996, and our suggestions for improving future action plans. The second contains our recommendations to Economic Leaders in the areas of cross-border flows, financial and investment issues, and economic and technical cooperation.

Some of our recommendations are new, while others build upon or refine proposals we made in our 1996 Report. Many are especially geared to the problems faced by small and medium-sized enterprises (SMEs).

REVIEW OF MAPA

Regarding ABAC's assessment of the Manila Action Plan for APEC, or MAPA, ABAC is well aware that APEC plans continuously to update and improve its action plans in the coming years. We welcome this intention and in assessing MAPA our primary goal has been offering recommendations for improving future action plans. These action plans constitute the essential link between APEC's grand vision of trade liberalization and the actual implementation by individual members that so crucially affects business.

SALOMON INC

From a business perspective, we found that the initial individual action plans compiled in MAPA are quite vague, non-transparent, and often lack specifics about what actions member economies plan to take to reach the APEC goal of free regional trade and investment by 2010 or 2020.

APEC members need to be more specific about how they intend to fulfill their commitments with respect to tariff and non-tariff barriers. Many of the action plans fail to offer additional commitments with regard to tariff and non-tariff barriers beyond what members have already promised in the WTO or other multilateral organizations.

With respect to services, ABAC encourages APEC to take a leading role in bringing the WTO financial services talks to a successful conclusion this year and, in the medium term, take a comprehensive approach to removing impediments across the full range of service industries. In the critical area of foreign direct investment, ABAC found very little in the MAPA by way of specific commitments to remove barriers.

In general, while APEC has produced fine-sounding principles or descriptions of best practices, these non-binding collective principles are not being translated into concrete action by individual members. We hope to see a more aggressive, action-oriented approach in the future.

Economic and technical cooperation, or ecotech, is another key pillar of APEC. ABAC's review found that many of APEC's existing ecotech activities have little relevance to business needs. At the same time, APEC's 1996 Declaration of Strengthening Economic and Technical Cooperation is a welcome initiative that could contribute to focusing and strengthening these disparate activities and making them more relevant. ABAC believes that it is critical that this Ministerial Declaration be rigorously implemented.

SALOMON INC

RECOMMENDATIONS TO LEADERS

ABAC will formally recommend that the Economic Leaders of APEC endorse the adoption by APEC of steps that will help capital markets facilitate economic growth. Specifically, we have put forth recommendations addressing currency instability, promoting regulation and transparency, establishing modern clearing and settlement systems, developing understandable and harmonized accounting standards and disclosure, broadening the local investor base, and liberalizing foreign access. We urge the Economic Leaders to endorse public-private sector cooperation to facilitate the development of markets for asset-backed securities in the region.

Additionally, in the area of cross-border flows, our Report offers specific proposals to facilitate business travel, improve enforcement of intellectual property rights, harmonize standards for business-related professional services, and establish more open, competitive government procurement systems. These recommendations are aimed at reducing the costs of cross-border business in the APEC region.

The Report also expresses support for APEC efforts to identify sectors for early, voluntary liberalization. Some examples of sectors where ABAC believes early action might occur include chemicals, environmental projects and services, food, oilseeds, pharmaceuticals, pulp and wood products, toys, and automotive and other transport products.

In the area of finance, investment and infrastructure, ABAC's recommendations are aimed at promoting more private investment in infrastructure, developing the region's capital markets, easing financing for small and medium-sized companies, and developing tax treaties to eliminate double taxation of firms that operate in more than one APEC economy.

The region's critical infrastructure needs can only be met if we enhance private investment in large-scale infrastructure projects in the region. For APEC to respond effectively to this need, we recommend a sectoral approach to

SALOMON INC

investment liberalization for infrastructure, through an Infrastructure Investment Initiative (III). The III applies enhanced investment protection on a sectoral basis to infrastructure projects. This builds on our APEC Voluntary Investment Project (AVIP) proposal last year for APEC to encourage a strong system of investment protection measures on a project-by-project basis. Under the III, APEC economies would be encouraged to apply a strong regime of investment protection measures to the infrastructure sector generally in order to attract more private investment.

Recent market instability is a very serious issue that is of high concern to ABAC members. Business needs a predictable macroeconomic environment, including stable foreign exchange markets. Relatively free-flowing international capital has been a key ingredient in the APEC region's economic success. Such openness, however, places an extra premium on sound macroeconomic management by economies. ABAC hopes that APEC economies will cooperate on this issue, which should include developing transparent and timely national economic statistics to provide early warning of macro economic imbalances, collective review of members' macro economic policies, developing and enforcing rules against market manipulation, developing and administering appropriate adjustment funds in cooperation with the IMF, and continuing financial sector liberalization.

Finally, ABAC has recommended two new initiatives: the Partnership for Equitable Growth and the Information Technology Education Initiative. The Partnership for Equitable Growth would be a non-profit organization that would identify, evaluate and provide funding to suitable ecotech projects that would benefit from close private-public cooperation. The Information Technology Education Initiative would involve the business and private sector to provide training in areas critical to information technology development.

All of ABAC's recommendations are offered in a constructive spirit and in response to Leaders' and Ministers' requests for business views on ways to

SALOMON INC

strengthen APEC. Leaders have recognized business as the "driving force for regional development." ABAC members appreciate and agree with that characterization and hope that APEC governments will act on it by implementing ABAC's recommendations. We firmly believe that doing so would expand trade and investment within APEC, promote regional development more broadly, and increase business support for the APEC process.

SIGNIFICANCE OF "FAST TRACK"

For the U.S. to continue to play a leadership role in groupings such as APEC, it is essential that we get a renewal of "Fast Track" trade negotiating authority. Trade liberalization and a stable investment environment benefits U.S. workers and U.S. businesses and creates markets for U.S. exports. Through new trade negotiations, the U.S. will continue to lead the APEC economies towards further trade liberalizing policies with the elimination of some of the same trade and financial access barriers that are being discussed today. Without "Fast Track" authority, U.S. leadership on trade and a broad range of other international economic issues would be impossible.

CONCLUSION

As a member of ABAC, I look forward to the opportunity to exchange views with the APEC Leaders in Vancouver and have appreciated this opportunity for dialogue on this issue with Congress. I also look forward to continuing to work with you on international trade and financial services issues and policy.

**TESTIMONY SUBMITTED
TO THE
COMMITTEE ON INTERNATIONAL RELATIONS
SUBCOMMITTEE ON ASIA AND THE PACIFIC**

**BY
J. BENNETT JOHNSTON
PRESIDENT, US-PECC
PACIFIC ECONOMIC COOPERATION COUNCIL**

NOVEMBER 6, 1997

APEC'S STRATEGY FOR TRADE LIBERALIZATION[1]

Introduction

The intergovernmental organization on APEC (Asia Pacific Economic Cooperation) has begun to implement the concept of "concerted unilateral liberalization" as the modality by which the Asia Pacific region will work towards achieving the goal of free and open trade and investment in the region by a date certain. This modality has not been applied anywhere else and is novel even to the Asia Pacific region. It is, however, a consistent manifestation of the understanding about the kind of regionalism that has emerged in the Asia Pacific. This regionalism is characterized by market integration (rather than institutional integration), the involvement of economies at different stages of development (rather than only among economies with similar levels of development), and its outward orientation (rather than inward orientation).

"Open regionalism" has become the defining concept of Asia Pacific regionalism. In the Asia Pacific region, as originated by PECC in its San Francisco Declaration of 1992 and articulated by Ross Garnaut (1996), open regionalism means regional economic integration without discrimination against outsiders. In the realm of APEC trade liberalization, this implies extending the liberalization on an unconditional Most Favored Nation (MFN) basis. From the outset, it has been envisaged that as a consultative forum APEC's contribution to trade liberalization in the region is by reinforcing and continuous encouragement of the efforts that are *unilaterally* undertaken by member economies. This is the essence of concerted unilateral liberalization.

Non-discriminatory regional initiatives are thought to be readily applicable to *trade and investment facilitation.* Trade facilitation is an important means whereby regional initiatives can benefit participants without excluding outsiders from the benefits. The APEC process in this area is particularly useful in augmenting private exchanges by providing some public goods to reduce international transactions costs. The first APEC meeting in 1989 clearly and rightly placed trade facilitation at the center of the regional agenda.

[1] This document is adapted from the background paper by Dr. Hadi Soesastro for the Twelfth General Meeting of the Pacific Economic Cooperation Council (PECC) in Santiago, Chile, September 29-October 1, 1997.

APEC has formally adopted the principle of open regionalism in its Seoul Declaration of 1991, although at that time it did not provide an operational definition of the concept. It is clear, however, that the spirit of regionalism as embodied in APEC, which presents itself clearly at the time of its inception in 1989, arises out of a deep concern over the fate of the global, multilateral trading regime and the slow progress of multilateral trade negotiations in the Uruguay Round of the GATT. Asia Pacific economies clearly recognized their great stake in the continuation of an open trading system. In light of this, open regionalism incorporates notions of being outward-looking, trade liberalizing, and GATT consistent.

The importance of keeping regionalism open in the Asia Pacific appears to have crystallized in the late 1980s, but the concept of open regionalism began to develop much earlier. It is not merely a response to perceived external (international) developments but results from an in-depth assessment of the nature of integration in the region. Open regionalism is also seen as a practical necessity for the region in view of the region's great diversities. It needs to be underlined over an over again that Asia Pacific economic cooperation and integration, as manifested in the APEC process, is not merely an exercise in trade and investment liberalization. It is first and foremost about *community building*. In view of the region's great diversities, community building will have to be guided by three important principles, namely: openness, equality, and evolution. *Openness* reflects the principle of open regionalism, which implies that decisions should be transparent and non-discriminatory. *Equality* implies that activities should be mutually beneficial to all participants. *Evolution* reflects a gradual, pragmatic and sustained process of voluntary cooperation based on consensus building (PECC, 1995).

Concerted Unilateral Liberalization

The wisdom of adopting an approach towards community building based on the above three principles was agreed upon as early as September 1980 at the Pacific Community Seminar in Canberra, which launched the non-governmental, tri-partite process known as PECC (Pacific Economic Cooperation Conference, later changed into the Pacific Economic Cooperation Council). The Seminar's recommendation encompasses the following principles for cooperation: (a) the need to avoid military and security issues so as to create a sense of community without creating a sense of threat; (b) an EEC-type discriminatory trading arrangement is inappropriate in the Pacific; (c) the need to "hasten slowly", and to proceed towards long-term goals step by step; (d) the need to ensure that existing bilateral, regional and global mechanism for cooperation are not undermined by any new wider regional arrangement and that it be complementary with them; (e) the need to ensure that it is an outward-looking arrangement; (f) the need for an "organic approach", building up private arrangements already existent in the Pacific; (g) the need to involve academics, businessmen and governments jointly in this cooperative enterprise; (h) the need to avoid unnecessary bureaucratic structures; (i) the need for a fairly loose and as far as possible non-institutionalized structure; (j) the need for all members to be placed on an equal footing; and, (k) the need to concentrate attention on areas of mutual regional interest.

In 1992 at its San Francisco meeting PECC issued a Declaration on "Open Regionalism: A Pacific Model for Global Economic Cooperation" which contains a precise formulation of the concept of open regionalism. The underlying premises of this Declaration are three-fold, namely: (1) that openness in the region is one of the main reasons for its economic dynamism; (2) that this openness complements the multilateral system; and, (3) that by making an explicit commitment to a model for open regionalism, the region can both continue its progress and make an important long-term contribution to a stronger, more open global economic system. Open regionalism not only recognizes regional realities but is also *consistent with the region's overriding interest in a rules-based multilateral trading system*.

The Declaration further elaborates on the conditions that define an open region, namely that: (a) economies in the region must increasingly remove barriers to trade, investment and technology flows; (b) they must apply GATT disciplines; (c) the region must provide commercial access to economies elsewhere and seek to ensure that these economies likewise provide commercial access on a *non-discriminatory* basis; and, (d) liberalizing sub-regional trading arrangements within the region must be accomodated. The above clearly shows that the Asia Pacific region deliberately opts for non-negotiated forms of economic integration and is opposed to discriminatory regionalism.

As described by Ross Garnaut (1996), there are three reasons why the region has avoided discrimination. The first reason is a practical one. If the region were to undertake regional trade liberalization through a conventional, discriminatory free trade area that is sanctioned by the GATT (WTO), it will have to meet certain conditions, namely substantial elimination of tariffs over a reasonable time period. It was thought that such conditions would not be attainable within the region because negotiating them would take a long time and would be highly divisive. Therefore, this would not be conducive to community building. For the Asia Pacific region this is the most compelling reason. Recent experience has also shown that its adoption by APEC has allowed the region to embark on an agenda for attaining "free and open trade and investment in the region" much earlier than expected and perhaps with greater success than would have been accomplished through negotiations.

The second reason is that the trading interests of the regional economies extend beyond the APEC region. A conventional free trade area would introduce detrimental tensions into trade relations with the rest of the world, and deter internationally-oriented reform and growth in the region's developing and transitional economies. The third reason is that trade discrimination introduces uncessary costs of trade diversion.

APEC's trade liberalization agenda has evolved and taken shape as a result of ongoing discussions on the operationalization of the concept of open regionalism. In the course of the discussion, the concept has been occasionally blurred or broadened to allow for some discrimination. The recommendations of the APEC Eminent Persons Groups (EPG, 1994), for instance, practically endorsed a negotiated free trade area and whose benefits will be extended to non-members only on a mutually reciprocal basis. Despite the suggestion that this modified modality could overcome the concerns about free-riding, especially by the Europeans, the original, precise meaning of open regionalism has survived.

Open regionalism in its precise meaning, as adopted by APEC in its meeting in Osaka in 1996, is consistent with the *voluntary* nature of the APEC process. It places great emphasis on and seeks to reinforce the process of unilateral liberalization that is being driven by the self-interests of its member economies. As such, liberalization commitments by member economies are not seen or treated as concessions. Concerted unilateral liberalization, is also consistent with Article 1 of the GATT (WTO) and this regional liberalization initiative does not need a formal Article 24 agreement.

Equally important, especially with a view on community building, is the sense of comfort that this modality provides to member economies as it allows them sufficient *flexibility* in implementing their liberalization commitments which are not based on negotiated schedules. In essence, APEC's trade liberalization and facilitation agenda is adopted and implemented by coordinated decisions of individual governments. Each member economy announces its own liberalization programs voluntarily, in accordance with the common guidelines for APEC cooperation which are adopted by consensus. These unilateral efforts are being concerted through consultation within APEC and their actual implementation will be monitored and reviewed jointly. As agreed upon in Osaka, member economies will submit individual action plans (IAPs), covering both trade liberalization and trade and investment facilitation measures. This is one, major element of the APEC trade liberalization agenda. The other element consists of collective action plans (CAPs). In the realm of trade liberalization, this can involve the adoption of non-discriminatory sectoral liberalization, covering, for instance, sectors in which regional economies trade intensively with each other. In its most recent meeting in Manila, APEC governments have agreed on an initiative to liberalize trade in information technologies which led to the adoption of an Information Technology Agreement (ITA) at the following WTO Ministerial Meeting in Singapore at the end of 1996. The ITA is also seen as an example of yet another element of APEC trade liberalization, namely the adoption of joint approaches or trade liberalization initiatives in wider multilateral or other fora.

APEC's Achievements To Date

The inaugural APEC ministerial meeting in Canberra in 1989 agreed on the basic principles of APEC. Firstly, APEC's objective is to sustain growth and development in the region and to contribute to growth of the world economy. Secondly, APEC should seek to strengthen an open multilateral trading system and not to be directed towards the formation of a regional trading bloc. Thirdly, APEC should focus on economic issues to advance common interests and foster constructive interdependence by encouraging the flow of goods, services, capital and technology. The meeting was attended by 26 ministers from 12 economies, namely the six ASEAN countries, South Korea, Japan, Australia, New Zealand Canada and the United States.

The following meeting, in Singapore in 1990, established seven work projects. They are meant to develop the habit of cooperation and to demonstrate the benefits of economic cooperation through such activities as improving regional data on the flow of goods, services and investment, enhancing technolofy transfer and human resources development, promoting cooperation in energy, and in marine resources, as well as in telecommunication. Later on three additional work projects were added: transportation, tourism, and fisheries. The establishment of these ten work projects was a significant development in APEC as they act to promote the development of regional networks among various governmental agencies as well as relevant non-governmental institutions. At this meeting APEC ministers issued a declaration stating their firm commitment to a timely and succesful completion of the Uruguay Round to demonstrate APEC's support for a strong, open multilateral system. The meeting also agreed that following the completion of the Uruguay Round, APEC would explore the scope for non-discriminatory regional trade liberalization.

The third meeting, which was held in Seoul in 1991, adopted the Seoul Declaration which sets out the scope of activity, mode of operation of, and the principles for participation in APEC. APEC's scope of activity includes: (a) exchange of information and consultation on relevant economic policies; (b) development of strategies to reduce impediments to trade and investment; and, (c) promotion of economic and technical cooperation. The Declaration explicitly stated that APEC's mode of operation is based on mutual benefit, a commitment to open dialogue and consensus building, and cooperation through consultation and exchange of views. In addition, APEC welcomes the participation of the private sector in relevant APEC activities. Following intensive diplomatic efforts by the host government, the meeting agreed to admit China, Hong Kong and Taiwan (as Chinese Taipei) as members. This was another significant development in APEC.

The following meeting, in Bangkok in 1992, marked the beginning of an institutionalization of the process. The meeting agreed to set up a permanent International Secretariat, located in Singapore, and an APEC Central Fund to finance APEC activities. The ministers reiterated APEC's firm commitment to a succesful completion of the Uruguay Round. They also confirmed the adoption of regional trade liberalization as one of the main priorities for the following year. A Committee on Trade and Investment (CTI) was established. The APEC process gained a further momentum at the fifth meeting in Seattle in 1993 when APEC admitted Mexico and Papua New Guinea as members. A decision was made to admit Chile in 1994 but to defer consideration of additional members for three years to allow the organization sufficient time for consolidation.

The meeting in Seattle elevated the process of cooperation to the highest level of government. At the proposal of the US President, Clinton, an APEC informal leaders meeting was held in conjuction with the ministerial meeting. The leaders issued an Economic Vision Statement which contains three main components. The first is an affirmation of the importance of an open multilateral trading system and the determination of Asia Pacific leaders to lead the way in taking concrete steps to produce the strongest possible outcome of the Uruguay Round.

The second component is a vision of *a community of Asia Pacific economies*: (a) which is based on the spirit of openness and partnership; (b) whose dynamic economic growth contributes to an expanding world economy and supports an open international trading system; (c) where trade and investment barriers continue to be reduced; (d) where the benefits of economic growth are shared by the people: (e) where education and training are improved; (f) where goods and people move quickly and efficiently because of advances in transportation and telecommunication; and, (g) where environment protection is improved to ensure sustainable growth and to provide a more secure future for the people.

The third element is a list of initiatives, which includes among others, the convening of meeting of APEC finance ministers, of APEC ministers involved with small and medium business enterprises, the establishment of a Pacific Business Forum, and the development of a non-binding code of principles covering investment issues.

The APEC leaders meeting the following year, held in Bogor (Indonesia) in 1994, produced the Bogor Declaration of Common Resolve which set the goal of free and open trade and investment in the region by no later than the year 2020. The commitment by leaders to achieve free and open trade at a date certain was an important milestone in APEC's development. The Declaration stipulates the principles for achieving the APEC goal, namely that it will be pursued promptly by further reducing barriers to trade and investment and by promoting the free flow of goods, services and capital among APEC economies, be achieved in a GATT-consistent manner, take into consideration the differing levels of economic development among APEC economies, with the industrialized economies achieving the goal no later than the year 2010 and developing economies no later than the year 2020. Furthermore, it states that APEC opposes the creation of an inward-looking trading bloc that would divert from the pursuit of global free trade and that the APEC goal will be pursued in a manner that will encourage and strengthen trade and investment liberalization globally.

Inspite of the principles contained in the Declaration there were some uncertainties as to the modality for achieving the APEC goal of free and open trade and investment in the region. There were proposals, including by the APEC EPG, which if implemented would amount to a process of negotiated liberalization among APEC members along a conventional free trade area, and whose benefits can be extended to non-members only on a mutually reciprocal basis. At issue here was the question of applying the principle of reciprocity to eliminate the problem of *free riding*, either within APEC itself or by non-members, Europe in particular.

The task of clarifying these issues rested with Japan, the 1995 chair of APEC. The meeting in Osaka was a close call. There were concerns that Japan would not be able to provide the necessary leadership to craft a meaningful road map for implementing the Bogor Declaration. However, Japan succesfully led the group to reaching a consensus by producing an Action Agenda and, as argued by Noordin Sopiee (1995), brought the APEC process *back on track*.

APEC has taken a broad view of the nature of free and open trade and investment. The so-called Osaka Action Agenda indicates that this will involve the elimination of all border barriers to trade and investment and the further reduction of all other impediments to international economic transactions. The 15 areas of cooperation contained in the Agenda include the removal of tariff and non-tariff barriers to trade in goods and services and reducing the costs and risks of international commerce caused by inadequate communications, partly due to infrastructure constraints, inadequate information about opportunities and uncertainty about future policies, as well as the divergent approaches to many domestic economic policies.

APEC participants have not ceded any powers of regulation or enforcement to any supra-national regional authority. Consequently, there are no *APEC decisions* as such. Decisions taken at APEC meetings are *decisions of APEC governments*. Since cooperation is voluntary, the many reforms that will be needed to reach the APEC goal will depend on policy decisions of individual governments. APEC's flexible approach makes it possible for Asia Pacific governments to set their own priorities and schedule for liberalization, allowing the process as a whole to make early headway.The guiding principles of the Osaka Action Agenda are designed to maximize the potential advantages of flexible and voluntary cooperation. The Osaka meeting agreed to adopt a set of nine principles, namely comprehensiveness, WTO-consistency; comparability; non-discrimination; tranparency; standstill; simultaneous start, continuos process and differentiated timetables; flexibility; and, cooperation.

It is important for the APEC process to view the above principles in the context of Asia Pacific regionalism as discussed above (see Drysdale, Elek, Soesastro, 1997). The principles of *comprehensiveness* combined with *flexibility* confirm that while participants can determine the sequence of their policy adjustments, "sensitive" sectors and policy issues will not be excluded from the agreed target dates for free and open trade and investment. The principle of *cooperation* reflects the reality that economic and technical cooperation to pool information, experience, expertise and technology will be vital to achieving region-wide engagement in many opportunities for facilitating trade and investment. In turn, they will help strengthen the capacities in the developing APEC members that would enhance their abilities to meet the APEC goal.

The principles concerning *comparability, standstill, simultaneous start, continuous process and differentiated timetables*, and *flexilibity* reflect political realities. While the dismantling of impediments to economic transactions among Asia Pacific economies is to be comprehensive, it is expected that most governments will leave what they preceive to be the most difficult political decisions to the later stages of the transition to free and open trade and investment. At the same time, for APEC to be credible, it is essential that all participants begin and sustain steady progress towards the agreed 2010 and 2020 targets. Hence the principle of simulataneous start and standstill, the latter ensuring that the dismantling of some obstacles to economic integration will not be accompanied by raising of others.

The principle of *comparability*, if viewed positively, reflects the intention of each APEC government to use the evidence of liberalization and facilitation by other APEC economies as arguments to counter domestic interests that oppose reforms. Such domestic political debates will be easier to win if governments can point out that all APEC governments are taking political decisions of comparable difficulty in their shared interest in moving towards the APEC goal. On the other hand, too much emphasis on the "comparability" of IAPs could divert scarce time and could become divisive. At worst, discussions among representatives of APEC governments could degenerate into GATT-style negotiations, where actions which would benefit an economy come to be regarded as costs.

The principle of *transparency, WTO-consistency* and *non-discrimination* are designed to maximize the benefits of cooperation as well as to ensure that cooperative arrangements among APEC economies take account of the interests of other economies. The principle of non-discrimination has been expressed as:

> APEC economies will apply or endeavour to apply the principle of non-discrimination between and among them in the process of liberalization and facilitation of trade and investment.
> The outcome of trade and investment liberalization in the Asia Pacific region will be the actual reduction of barriers not only among APEC economies but also between APEC economies and non-economies.

The first part of the principle of non-discrimination recognizes that community buidling in the region and the cohesion of APEC depends on avoiding, as far as possible, creating new sources of discrimination among APEC economies. The second underlines APEC's commitment to open regionalism. Both represent pragmatic compromises. The first recognizes that many APEC economies belong to preferential sub-regional trading arrangements and that under current legislation, the United States cannot guarantee unconditional MFN treatment of trade with China. Consistently with the concept of open regionalism, the second part of the non-discrimination principle confirms that APEC economies will reduce impediments to trade and investment with respect to non-participants. It also reflects the concern of some participants that if APEC market-opening were extended equally to all other economies, it could encourage free riding, particularly by European economies.

The above guiding principles have proved adequate to initiate the start of substantive, practical cooperation among member economies. In Manila, at the seventh APEC meeting, all members submitted their IAPs and they have agreed on a series of CAPs. The IAPs and CAPs were examined and discussed by APEC officials throughout 1996 under the chairmanship of the Philippines. Although there were no negotiations, there was significant "peer pressure" on all governments that encourage them to make greater commitments in order to boost confidence in the capacity of the voluntary process of cooperation.

The individual and collective actions that form the Manila Action Plan for APEC (MAPA) relate to the three pillars of APEC: trade and investment liberalization; facilitation; and economic and technical cooperation. An independent assessment undertaken by PECC concluded that individual APEC economies are *all* well on track towards the Bogor goal and that in many cases tariff reductions are faster and deeper than the commitments made under the Uruguay Round. As can be seen from Table 1, the process has contributed to a lowering of tariffs in the region. The average (unweighted) tariff level has been lowered from 15 percent in 1988 to 9 percent in 1996. A number of economies (Chile, China, Korea, Philippines and Thailand) experienced a dramatic reduction in their average tariff levels. Some other economies (Chile, China, Indonesia and the Philippines) have made tariff reduction commitments so that they are set to move ahead in achieving their Bogor target (PECC, 1996)

In addition, the IAPs have begun to address non-tariff measures. All APEC members have made a submission to reduce NTBs and most members have made a general commitment to review NTBs with a view to reduce or eliminate those NTBs that are not consistent with the WTO measures. Some economies (Australia, China, Hong Kong, Indonesia, Japan, Korea, the Philippines and PNG) offered detailed liberalization measures.

Table 1 Unweighted Average Tariffs of APEC economics, 1988 - 1996

	1988	1993	1996
Australia	15.6	9.0	6.1
Brunei	3.9	3.9	2.0
Canada	9.1	8.8	6.7
Chile	19.9	14.9	10.9
China	40.3	37.5	23.0
Hong Kong	0.0	0.0	0.0
Indonesia	20.3	17.0	13.1
Japan	7.2	6.5	9.0
Korea	19.2	11.6	7.9
Malaysia	13.0	12.8	9.0
Mexico	10.6	12.8	12.5
New Zealand	15.0	8.0	7.0
Philippines	27.9	23.5	15.6
Singapore	0.4	0.4	0.0
Chinese Taipei	12.6	8.9	8.6
Thailand	40.8	37.8	17.0
USA	6.6	6.6	6.4
Average	15.4	12.9	9.1

Source: PECC (1996)

On the liberalization of services trade, MAPA includes among other things: an explicit statement of support for the WTO negotiating processes on services trade liberalization; unilateral actions by some economies which go beyond their WTO schedules, especially with respect to services firms' offshore establishment; commitments to collective APEC action to support WTO negotiations on professional services and on telecommunications; and, the adoption of sets of APEC principles for the development of open markets for energy services and telecommunications.

In the area of investments, some APEC members have committed to undertake liberalization measures, but progress here has been rather disappointing (Bora and Graham, 1997). Other commitments were made including in the area of facilitation and economic and technical cooperation. These too have not been as significant as those in the area of trade liberalization. In view of the fact that this process has entered only its first round, further initiatives in the many other areas covered by the MAPA may be taken in subsequent rounds.

Challenges Ahead

Thus far MAPA has brought APEC much farther in its progress towards meeting the APEC goal formulated in Bogor as well as promoting community building in the region. Nonetheless, APEC still face the challenge of being able to sustain this voluntary and flexible process. It needs to be recognized that the voluntary and flexible nature of APEC carry some risks.

While simultaneous action is not needed for liberalizing traditional border barriers to trade or investment, some governments may be tempted to slow the pace of reform if others are also holding back. In the area of facilitation, encouraging some to move ahead of others can set positive examples, but could also sow the seeds of division and confusion if cooperative arrangement among some APEC economies neglect, or damage, the interests of others. In short, this process cannot be taken for granted.

APEC needs to devise mechanisms that would help keep the momentum going. A continuous review and monitoring process of the implementation of the Osaka Action Agenda (MAPA and beyond) by individual APEC members is of critical importance. In view of nature of its organization and its extensive network, PECC is in an ideal position to contribute to this process by offering its independent assessments of the progress on a regular basis.

APEC should also begin to develop principles and modalities to implement cooperative arrangements to facilitate trade and investment on the basis of open regionalism. It is likely that as APEC deepens its cooperation agenda it may have to allow for different speeds in its facilitation efforts. For most options to facilitate trade or investment, the more economies involved the greater the benefits to all of them. It would make sense, therefore, to encourage region-wide involvement from the outset. However, it would be counter-productive to insist that all APEC participants be involved in every specific initiative for cooperation. Thus, it is imperative for APEC to devise ways to ensure that cooperative arrangements involving some (not all) APEC economies take careful account of the interests of others and promote the smooth evolution of region-wide arrangements.

Drysdale, Elek and Soesastro (1997) have outlined a concise set of principles for the design of such cooperative arrangements as follows.

> *APEC economies that are ready to initiate and implement cooperative arrangements to reduce impediments to economic transactions are encouraged to do so, while taking account of the interests of other economies as follows:*
>
> *Transparency:*
> *(I) The policies adopted to implement these arrangements should be documented explicitly (typically expressed in legislation or regulations of those economies) and be freely available and accessible, through convenient channels of communication.*
>
> *(ii) APEC economies should provide reasonable prior notice of the nature and objectives of proposed cooperative arrangements as well as the policies by which these are to be implemented.*
>
> *Non-discrimination:*
> *The arrangements should not contain any provisions which result in new or additional discrimination, either against products on the basis of the location of production, or among producers on the basis of their place of registration or ownership.*
>
> *Accession:*
> *(I) Any economy whose government accepts the responsibilities as well as the benefits of following policies compatible with any existing or proposed*

cooperative arrangements among some APEC economies should be able to, and encouraged to, become parties to these arrangements.

(ii) Existing parties to these cooperative arrangements should be willing to share the information, experience, expertise and technology needed to enable others to adopt the relevant policies.

Review:
APEC economies should endeavor to respond positively to constructive suggestions from other economies for improving the consistency of existing or proposed cooperative arrangements with APEC's agreed guiding principles for trade and investment liberalization and facilitation.

Cooperative arrangements which met all of these criteria could be appropriately described as *open clubs*. The adoption of the principles of open clubs could avoid the proliferation of arrangements that fragment, rather than integrate, regional markets. As trade and investment facilitation should go hand in hand with trade and investment liberalization, this modality of facilitation activities should be adopted in parallel with concerted unilateral liberalization.

References

Bora, Bijit and Graham, Edward M. (1997), *Can APEC Deliver on Investment?* Centre for International Economic Studies, University of Adelaide, Policy Discussion paper No. 97/08 (J·une).

Drysdale, Peter; Elek, Andrew and Soesastro, Hadi (1997), *Open Regionalism: The Nature of Asia Pacific Integration*, paper presented at a CEPR/ESRC/GEI Conference on Europe, East Asia, APEC and the Asia-Europe Meeting (ASEM) Process, London (20-21 May).

Garnaut, Ross (1996), *Open Regionalism and Trade Liberalization* (Singapore: ISEAS).

PECC (1995), "Beijing Statement on Open Regionalism for Global Prosperity" *PECC Memorandum* (September)

PECC (1996) in cooperation with PIDS and The Asia Foundation, *Perpectives on the Manila Action Plan for APEC.*

Sopiee, Noordin (1995), "Getting APEC Back on Track," *The Asian Wall Street Journal,* 14 November.

APPENDIX

"ASSESSMENT OF THE MANILA ACTION PLAN FOR APEC"
BACKGROUND REPORT FOR THE APEC BUSINESS
ADVISORY COUNCIL PREPARED BY THE PACIFIC ECONOMIC
COOPERATION COUNCIL (PECC) TRADE POLICY FORUM.
JUNE, 1997.

APEC AT VANCOUVER: THE FINANCE SUMMIT

Statement by

C. Fred Bergsten

Director, Institute for International Economics*

Subcommittee on Asia and the Pacific
Committee on International Relations
US House of Representatives

November 6, 1997

At its summit meeting in Vancouver on November 25, the Asia Pacific Economic Cooperation (APEC) forum should launch new arrangements to help prevent and respond to future monetary crises in the region. There is a clear need for such arrangements and APEC is the logical institutional home for the "Asian Monetary Fund" that has been discussed so widely since the onset of the current financial problems in Southeast Asia.

The primary goal would be prevention of future crises. After Mexico exploded in early 1995, there were extensive efforts to improve the "early warning system." But that system failed again in Thailand. Moreover, the contagion to neighboring countries is far worse now than in Latin America in 1995.

The International Monetary Fund (IMF) did its job in foreseeing and warning of the impending problem. The systemic problem was that Thailand balked and no one pressed it to act.

The IMF on its own demonstrably cannot get emerging economies to adjust preemptively. It is unlikely that the industrial countries as a group, through the Group of Seven, or individual powers like the United States or Japan can do so. The best prospect is neighboring countries: because they are so likely to be hurt themselves by fallout from a crisis, their intervention is both legitimate and apt to be delivered forcefully.

APEC can provide the institutional locus for such efforts. It is already developing a process of "peer pressure" or "friendly persuasion" through which individual members encourage others to act responsibly, in the interests of the broader group as well as their own. APEC is using this approach to pursue "free and open trade and investment in the region by 2010 (for the

---

* C. Fred Bergsten was also Chairman of APEC's Eminent Persons Group throughout its existence from 1993 through 1995.

advanced countries) or 2020 (for the rest)," the commitment undertaken at the Bogor summit in 1994. The most dramatic success came at last year's Subic summit when peer pressure persuaded a number of members to eliminate their tariffs on a wide range of high-tech products, enabling APEC to galvanize the Information Technology Agreement (ITA) on $500 billion of global trade in the World Trade Organization a few weeks later.

The APEC Finance Ministers have been meeting regularly since the Seattle summit in 1993 instructed them to do so. Their deputies have convened even more often, most recently during the IMF meetings in Hong Kong last month. They have already discussed the currency and related issues in depth. They should begin systematically assessing national economic outlooks and pressing members to adopt good advice, from the IMF and elsewhere, that would head off future crises and thereby avoid new disruption in the region.

APEC should also create a standby funding arrangement to support further IMF programs in the region. The current cases are only the latest reminders that such crises inevitably occur from time to time. International rescue packages will be required in the future as in the past.

It is also clear that IMF lending by itself will never be adequate. The IMF has plenty of money, including from the latest increases agreed at Hong Kong and the standby General Arrangements to Borrow and (when implemented) New Arrangements to Borrow. But IMF credits to any individual country are limited by that country's quota at the Fund; even the unprecedented multiples for Mexico (700 percent of quota) and Thailand (500 percent) produced only one-quarter to one-third of the amounts needed.

Widespread support has therefore developed for an "Asian Monetary Fund" to supplement the IMF. But Japan's proposal for an Asia-only facility was rejected by all concerned, including its intended beneficiaries, on a variety of grounds. ASEAN is obviously too small. The "Six Markets Group" (or G-6) that met last spring included the United States but excluded many key Asian countries.

APEC is the logical institutional venue for such arrangements. It includes all the Asian countries that might need help. It includes all the potential creditors, including the United States and Canada as well as Japan, China, Taiwan and Brunei. Its Latin American members would be helpful, Mexico with its crisis and dramatic recovery experience and Chile as a healthy role model. As noted, its Finance Ministers have already developed an extensive cooperative relationship and discussed the relevant issues at length.

The main criticism of this proposal is that any standing fund would create "moral hazard," the risk that its very existence would assure future bailouts and thereby tempt countries to pursue profligate policies and private investors to continue pouring money into unsustainable situations. But there is a decisive answer to this concern (which, in any event, is often simply an excuse from those who wish to avoid putting up money): to tie any APEC arrangements inextricably to IMF programs. No country would put itself through the wringer of a monetary crisis and subject itself to the tender mercies of the IMF simply because rescue funds were available. Nor would private investors keep coming, with countless alternative opportunities around the world, if the Fund requires them to share the costs of adjustment programs as it must.

Moreover, the alternative to standby arrangements is *ad hoc* bailouts as cobbled together by the United States for Mexico and Japan for Thailand. Their outcome is always highly uncertain, as when the Congress almost blocked the Mexican package. Their magnitude, sharing among donors and speed of delivery are purely fortuitous. Prepared standby funding is far preferable.

The APEC summiteers should thus launch new preventive and funding arrangements at Vancouver. In 1993, they decided to create "a community of Asia Pacific economies"; the community now requires better mechanisms to avoid and handle future crises. In 1994, they decided to achieve "free trade in the region"; they now need comparably bold initiatives on the financial side. In 1996, they effectively applied peer pressure to achieve the ITA; they now need to use similar techniques to head off monetary disruptions. Vancouver can be the "finance summit" that will add to this chain of dramatic successes and further mark APEC as the outstanding international institutional innovation of the post-Cold War era.

Ambassador John S. Wolf Testimony on APEC
Subcommittee on Asia and Pacific
November 6, 1997
Question for the Record
Submitted by Representative Bereuter
(Date of Question: December 8, 1997)

Question

Traditionally, the US has been against any free-trade agreements among Asian countries. We also opposed the East Asian Economic Caucus, or EAEC, proposed several years ago.

What is the Administration's feelings now regarding bilateral agreements between Asian states?

Answer

The U.S. has been supportive of bilateral free-trade agreements between Asian states, which we view as assisting the APEC-wide effort toward free and open trade, as long as they do not damage U.S. commercial interests. We have also been and remain supportive of regional agreements among Asian states -- the ASEAN Free Trade Area, for example.

I should stress here that the APEC push for free and open trade is aided not only by agreements on trade liberalization, but also by efforts toward trade facilitation. American business tells us that facilitation has a direct and positive impact on their bottom line. APEC can promote trade facilitation in a number of ways -- for example, by aiding business mobility and by coordinating and harmonizing technical standards among member economies. We therefore also support bilateral and regional efforts which assist APEC-wide trade facilitation.

Ambassador John S. Wolf Testimony on APEC
Subcommittee on Asia and Pacific
November 6, 1997
Question for the Record
Submitted by Representative Bereuter
(Date of Question: December 8, 1997)

Question

Membership in APEC is increasing, and currently there are a number of pending applications for consideration. At this time, there is a fair amount of support for admitting Vietnam and Peru into APEC.

What is the U.S. position on new members? If supportive, which countries would the U.S. like to see admitted next?

Answer

The U.S. supported the consensus among APEC Leaders in Vancouver on November 25 to admit three new members -- Vietnam, Peru, and Russia -- effective November 1998 at the APEC Ministerial and Leaders' Meetings in Kuala Lumpur. This will bring APEC membership to 21 economies.

APEC members want to preserve the informal nature of the organization, which will be diminished if it grows too large. For this reason, APEC Leaders in Vancouver agreed on a ten-year consolidation period after which membership issues will be considered further.

Ambassador John S. Wolf Testimony on APEC
Subcommittee on Asia and Pacific
November 6, 1997
Question for the Record
Submitted by Representative Bereuter
(Date of Question: December 8, 1997)

Question

In the past, APEC members have disagreed over the non-discrimination principle or what has been termed "open regionalism." Japan has pressed for the benefits of APEC trade liberalization to be accorded to even non-APEC trading partners on a most-favored-nation basis as Japan does not want APEC to become a trading bloc which discriminates against outsiders.

Could you please describe the U.S. position on the issue of non-discrimination? How can the United States ensure that our APEC trade liberalization commitments are not taken advantage of by free-riders?

Answer

The U.S. position is that regional trade liberalization within APEC can serve as a catalyst for global trade liberalization. The best way to pursue the Bogor goals of free and open trade and investment is to get a critical mass of support for a liberalization effort from among APEC economies, use that support as leverage to induce others to do the same, and in that way address concerns arising from non-discrimination.

It is illustrative that in Manila last year, only nine APEC members supported APEC work on an Information Technology Agreement (ITA). Now, more than forty countries, including the vast majority of APEC members and most other major U.S. trading partners, have signed on to the WTO Agreement on Information Technology.

The plan regarding the trade liberalization package coming out of Vancouver is to finalize the nine sector proposals by next June and begin implementation as soon as 1999. At the same time, the sector proposals will be taken to the WTO, as appropriate, for agreement with other trading partners, especially the European Union, and set as binding agreements in the manner of the ITA.

One more point: non-discriminatory trade liberalization efforts can serve another vital purpose, by sending signals to financial markets that the participating economies are confident and growth-minded, rather than retreating toward protectionism. This was exactly the case in Vancouver, where the APEC Leaders' endorsement of a meaningful liberalization package signaled that President Clinton and the other leaders were committed to sustained, secure growth in the region, and that the Asia-Pacific was not about to let itself degenerate into a trade war, despite recent set-backs in the financial sectors of some member economies.

Ambassador John S. Wolf Testimony on APEC
Subcommittee on Asia and Pacific
November 6, 1997
Question for the Record
Submitted by Representative Bereuter
(Date of Question: December 8, 1997)

Question

Up until now, the trade liberalization measures offered by most of the APEC members have been those already committed to as a result of the Uruguay Round. The time is approaching when APEC members will have to consider new initiatives beyond the Uruguay Round to achieve the goals of the Bogor Declaration

Is APEC as an institution capable of inducing trade liberalization beyond the Uruguay Round? Or is APEC more of a platform to generate support for proposals to be submitted to the WTO?

Answer

APEC's record shows it can lead trade liberalization in the WTO and can induce liberalization beyond the Uruguay Round.

APEC Leaders provided critical support for conclusion of the Uruguay Round at their first meeting in Seattle in 1993. APEC Leaders played a decisive role in bringing the WTO agreements on Information Technology and Basic Telecommunications to a successful conclusion in 1996.

At their meetings in Vancouver in November, APEC Ministers identified nine sectors that enjoyed the most support for early voluntary liberalization. These sectors (environmental goods and services, fish and fish products, forest products, medical equipment and instruments, energy, toys, gems and jewelry, chemicals, and a telecommunications mutual recognition arrangement) account for $1.5 trillion in worldwide trade. Work to liberalize these sectors will take place throughout 1998 and they will be implemented beginning in 1999. Six additional sectors were identified for liberalization some time after 1999. Agreements in these sectors will include market opening, facilitation and other cooperative measures. APEC will build on liberalization in these sectors to extend participation outside the Asia-Pacific region and, where appropriate, these sectors will be incorporated into the WTO.

Ambassador John S. Wolf Testimony on APEC
Subcommittee on Asia and Pacific
November 6, 1997
Question for the Record
Submitted by Representative Sherrod Brown
(Date of Question: December 8, 1997)

Question

Most of the flashlight companies in the U.S. have joined together to form the Flashlight Tariff Coalition to eliminate tariffs worldwide. The Coalition has actively requested that the Administration pursue flashlight tariff elimination in the Asia Pacific Economic Cooperation (APEC) forum.

High tariffs in other countries have hindered the growth of U.S. flashlight exports. Eveready Battery Company, for example, has several flashlight operations in Ohio which stand to benefit from the reduction or elimination of high tariffs in other nations, especially those in Latin America.

I understand, and am pleased, that the U.S. Trade Representative (USTR) has recognized flashlights as a possible candidate for early sectoral liberalization in APEC. The Coalition has sought tariff elimination in APEC, the Information Technology Agreement, the Trans-Atlantic Business Dialogue, and any other possible trade forum. Until this point, however, USTR has insisted that it does not have negotiating authority, and thus it has not pursued flashlight tariff elimination.

Is the U.S. now prepared to pursue tariff elimination on flashlights in APEC?

Answer

In Vancouver, APEC Ministers identified nine product sectors for immediate action to conclude liberalization, and six other sectors on which work could be developed. Sectors were considered and chosen on the basis of whether they had broad social and economic benefits, whether they were commercially significant, and whether they had broad support among APEC economies. Ministers sought a package that would contain mutually beneficial and balanced recommendations for liberalization.

In its consultations with the flashlight industry, U.S. negotiators made it clear that they would explore with other APEC economies whether those economies would support inclusion of flashlights as a sector for early liberalization. The United States, however, did not receive any indications of support from other economies, nor did it receive indications that other economies considered that flashlights met the criteria applicable to sectors chosen.

Still, the United States remains willing to continue working with industry consultants to find ways of relating flashlights to ongoing APEC liberalization efforts.

What to Expect from APEC this November in Vancouver?

by

Steve Parker
Chief Economist, The Asia Foundation, San Francisco
and, U.S. Coordinator, Trade Policy Forum
Pacific Economic Cooperation Council
October, 19, 1997

The Asia Pacific Economic Cooperation (APEC) Forum consists of 18 member economies surrounding the Pacific Ocean.[1] These diverse economies are pulled together by a common goal of creating a pacific community with prosperous economies, expanding trade and investment flows, and mutual understanding and respect. APEC's agenda has been pushed forward dramatically over the last four years, starting with President Clinton's Blake Island meeting of the leaders in 1993, followed dramatically by President Suharto's orchestration of the 1994 Bogor Declaration that called for all APEC economies to achieve free and open trade and investment by 2010 for developed economies and 2020 for developing economies. The Osaka Action Plan was developed in 1995 to provide a road map for achieving the Bogor objectives, reiterating APEC's commitment to full and comprehensive liberalization.

In 1996, under Philippines leadership, APEC broke new ground -- creating the Manila Action Plan for APEC (MAPA) where for the first time every APEC economy laid out concrete steps for how they would achieve the Bogor objectives, stimulating trade and investment liberalization and facilitation (TILF) through Individual Action Plans (IAPs) and Collective Action Plans (CAPs), and economic and technical cooperation (Ecotech) through a wide range of joint activities (fostered by a Ministerial Declaration on Economic and Technical Cooperation). APEC leaders also agreed last year to call for a major initiative to lower tariffs to zero on information technology products. An Information Technology Agreement (ITA) was accepted on a global bases shortly thereafter by the WTO at its Singapore Ministerial meeting in early December, 1996.

1997 has been a year of consolidation for APEC under Canadian leadership, working to strengthen and deepen its increasingly well formed work agendas. The leaders meeting, which has become the focus of the annual APEC process, is not expected to generate "spectaculars." Canada's leadership theme is organized around a call to expand infrastructure in the region and to enhance civil society participation in the APEC process, especially youth and women.

---

[1] APEC currently includes: Singapore, Malaysia, Indonesia, Thailand, Philippines, Brunei, China, Hong Kong, China, Chinese Taipei, Korea, Japan, Australia, New Zealand, Papua New Guinea, Canada, United States, Mexico and Chile.

It is not expected, for example, that the leaders will make any substantive announcements regarding the WTO negotiations on financial services that are scheduled for completion in December, nor on the Southeast Asia financial and currency situation. Similarly, leaders are not expected to promote an APEC view on the upcoming Kyoto Conference on Global Warming.

In line with the workmanlike nature of this year's APEC process, attention is likely to be focused more on a range of ministerial-level work. Most economies will be announcing improvements to their IAPs and CAPs, and the formats for these plans will be standardized to foster monitoring and comparing the implementation of commitments. Highlights of these improvements are expected to involve lower tariff and non-tariff levels spread over a number of economies and sectors, acceleration toward a paperless customs regime and improved harmonization of product standards and testing in the region, and streamlined business visas. Through this process, APEC is working to reduce many of the costs that businesses complain most about.

Probably the biggest surprise for the year has been the acceleration of the process to achieve early sectoral voluntary liberalization (ESVL) that was stimulated by a mid-term Ministers of Trade meeting in Montreal. Following on last year's dramatic precedent with the ITA, they have called for APEC to identify specific sectors for accelerated liberalization, including not only tariffs and non-tariff barriers, but also facilitation, infrastructure and human resource development needs. Over the year, APEC has established a procedure for voluntary submission of sectors and related policy reforms by each economy, and are currently working to achieve a critical mass of economies around specific sectors (key officials will be meeting in late October in Singapore for a special set of meetings to further this process). There is still considerable uncertainty regarding what this process will produce, and negotiations can be expected to continue right up to the Vancouver meeting deadlines. It is most likely, however, that a handful of sectors -- like fish and environmental products -- will be named for early liberalization. It is not clear, however, what the time frame will be, nor whether liberalization will be done on an unilateral, most-favored-nation basis or as an initiative for WTO action. It seems unlikely that ESVL will involve preferential regional schemes.

APEC has struggled with two "structural" issues -- management of the Ecotech activities and membership expansion. A number of economies in APEC, including developing economies such as China, have pushed to create a separate committee on Ecotech to heighten its prestige and mandate, and to improve its management and funding base. By all accounts, the Ecotech process has been unwieldy and lacking of focus. Ecotech activities are a fundamental innovation by APEC, acting to balance the needs of developing and developed economies in the region, to support implementation of reforms and the building of needed social and physical infrastructure to make those reforms effective, and to advance the underlying understanding and mutual respect required for a successful community to flourish. Although the 1996 Manila Declaration on Ecotech set an important benchmark, accommodating the desire for "focused outcomes" on one hand, with softer community building and development objectives on the other, has proven difficult. It appears unlikely that a major breakthrough on Ecotech will be accomplished by Vancouver.

Expanding APEC's membership has occupied a surprising amount of time, at the bureaucratic level and even among the leaders. At stake is the desire by some to solidify the APEC work agenda with a strong track record of accomplishment, given that it already includes an amazingly diverse set of economies while maintaining a comprehensive approach to TILF and Ecotech. And yet, a number of economies are pressuring hard to be invited into APEC, which has always promoted itself as an open and non-exclusive club. Agreement has been made this year to present clear guidelines for new membership selection, with specific economies named in 1998 for formal entry in 1999. Compromises are likely in this process, and there is some chance that several new members may even be announced ahead of schedule in Vancouver (leading candidates include Vietnam and Peru).

Although some fret about the expected low-key nature of this year's meetings in Vancouver, the APEC process remains alive and well. APEC needs to strengthen its internal processes and needs to move forcefully from rhetoric to action. APEC's success this year will be measured in terms of starting the process of concrete improvements in policy reform, facilitation, infrastructure and community building, laying a basis for ongoing broad-based economic prosperity in the region and resolution of inevitable disputes.

APEC's credibility will be questioned over time, however, unless these promised, pragmatic contributions are made and unless it can deal effectively with the many emerging issues that affect the region's economic performance. Looking beyond Vancouver, Malaysia will take over leadership of APEC in 1998 at a critical period when expectation and performance will be expected to meet. Although early indications are that Malaysia will stress Ecotech issues, especially human resource development, APEC will need ASEAN's typically dynamic leadership to push APEC forward on a number of fronts, including trade and investment liberalization and facilitation, and attention to emerging issues such as financial market development, currency policy and sustainable development.

STATEMENT OF

Marcus Noland
Senior Fellow
Institute for International Economics
11 Dupont Cir., NW
Washington, DC

HEARINGS ON

The Fifth Summit of the Asia Pacific Economic Cooperation Forum

6 November 1997

House International Relations Committee
Subcommittee on Asian and Pacific Affairs

The views expressed in this statement are those of the author and do not necessarily reflect the views of individual members of the Institute's Board of Directors or Advisory Committee.

The Fifth Summit of the Asia Pacific Economic Cooperation Forum

It is an honor to be invited to submit testimony to this Subcommittee. Regrettably, I am unable to appear before the Subcommittee in person, and would respectfully like to submit this written testimony. In it, I will make three main points:

- A number of Asian countries have relatively fragile financial systems, a problem that has been exacerbated by politicization and misuse of the financial system for political ends.
- The recent collapse in equity prices in these countries may not only adversely effect their own growth prospects in the medium-run, but the growth prospects of other countries as well.
- Successful resolution of these problems will require both narrow technocratic responses and broader political changes -- which may prove painful. The scope for US technical support is enormous, but the US should evaluate requests for financial assistance carefully. In this regard, the Asia Pacific Economic Cooperation (APEC) Forum may prove to be a useful instrument in bringing peer pressure to bear on governments in the region.

THE CAUSES OF FINANCIAL INSTABILITY IN ASIA

This year a number of countries in Asia have experienced significant nominal exchange rate depreciation and declines in asset prices. In Thailand the stockmarket has fallen by nearly half from its peak earlier in the year and the baht has depreciated more than 66 percent against the dollar since June. Other countries around the region have had similar experiences: in the Philippines the stock market is down by nearly half, and the currency 34 percent; in Malaysia the stock market is down 45 percent and the currency 33 percent; in Indonesia the stockmarket is down 33 percent and the currency 49 percent; and in South Korea, the stockmarket is down by more than 40 percent, and the won has depreciated 8 percent against the dollar. In China and Hong Kong the stock markets are down significantly, though their currencies have as yet remained firm against the dollar. Asset price declines have not been limited to the stockmarket: other asset prices (such as real estate prices) have fallen as well.

Although these results are disturbing, to some degree they are not wholly unexpected: developing countries (including those in Asia) exhibit more volatility in macroeconomic aggregates and financial market indicators than larger, more diversified, developed economies.[1] Greater volatility in rates of inflation and economic growth can hamper risk assessment by developing country financial institutions. Developing countries tend to have more institutionally concentrated financial systems than developed countries (i.e. fewer banks account for a larger share of lending). Moreover, these institutions themselves tend to hold less diversified portfolios than their counterparts in developed countries. A higher share of assets tends to be denominated in the domestic currency, and assets tend to be more concentrated in terms of sectoral distribution. For example, loans to the domestic real estate sector or construction companies make up a large share of the loan portfolios of many developing country banks. This relative lack of portfolio diversification tends to make the financial sectors of developing countries more fragile than those of developed countries. Although developing country banks may meet the same nominal capital adequacy standards as developed country banks, on a risk-adjusted basis many are undercapitalized,

---

[1] For evidence on this point, see Morris Goldstein and Philip Turner, "Banking Crises in Emerging Economies: Origins and Policy Options," *BIS Economic Papers*, No. 49, Basle: Bank for International Settlements, October 1996, Table 1.

creating vulnerability to economic downturns.[2]

In some cases financial fragility has been exacerbated by a mismatch of assets and liabilities by both financial sector and non-financial sector firms. For example, if domestic interest rates are high relative to foreign interest rates, banks may be tempted to finance long-term domestic lending through short-run foreign borrowing. This leaves them (and, by extension, domestic lending) vulnerable to either foreign interest rate spikes or domestic currency depreciation. This may be particularly problematic if the domestic currency is pegged to a foreign currency such as the dollar, and the peg is abandoned and the domestic currency depreciates.

Finally, domestic policy may contribute to financial fragility in at least two distinct ways. As noted earlier, developing country financial systems tend to be under-diversified. The presence of foreign financial institutions may effectively increase diversification and reduce fragility. For example, foreign banks tend to be less exposed to the host country's domestic economy, and thereby in a better position to maintain lending during downturns in which host country institutions may be far more negatively impacted. Lack of financial openness, therefore, can contribute to financial crises.

More fundamentally, domestic policy may contribute directly to financial crises by encouraging financial institutions to act in economically inefficient or irrational ways. For example, financial institutions may be encouraged to channel capital to politically connected or preferred borrowers to the detriment of the economy.[3] Such practices may be sustainable as long as the rate

---

[2] See Goldstein and Turner op. cit. Table 4.

[3] For a more detailed development of these ideas in the Korean context, see Marcus Noland, "Restructuring Korea's Financial System for Greater Competitiveness," *Working Paper Series*,

of economic growth remains high, as financial institutions compensate for the low effective rate of return on loans to these preferred borrowers with high rates of return on other loans. However, if the rate of growth slows, the bad loan drag begins to inhibit the ability of banks and non-bank lending institutions to supply credit to the economy. This is what has transpired in a number of Asian economies this year as prices declined in some key exports (computer chips, autos, and some light manufactures where Chinese exports have emerged rapidly, to cite a few examples). With the slowdown in export revenue, growth prospects diminished. Equity prices began to fall followed by movement out of the domestic currency leading to exchange rate depreciation (in countries that float their currency), or alternatively, pressure on the exchange rate peg (in countries that peg to a foreign currency like the dollar). Parenthetically, the movement out of domestic assets is typically led by domestic residents (not foreign speculators) and the available evidence (on net stock market purchases, for example) suggests that this was likely the pattern in the recent events in Asia as well.

Gauging the extent of current distress is difficult due to unconventional and opaque accounting practices in a number of countries, but private sector estimates of the amount of non-performing loans to national income among the developing countries of the region range from less than 5 percent in the case of Singapore, to 20-25 percent in the cases of Thailand, Malaysia, and South Korea. Put another way, South Korea appears to be facing a banking crisis on the scale of our saving and loan debacle -- but with an economy less than one tenth the size of ours, and without the cushion that a high level of per capita income provides.

96-14, Washington: Institute for International Economics; downloadable from www.iie.com

ECONOMIC IMPACT

The medium-run impact of these financial problems obviously differs from country to country around the region depending on the underlying economic fundamentals of each country, policy responses, and spillover effects. It would be beyond the scope of this testimony to analyze the economic circumstances of each country in the region. However, it should be noted that markets respond to government policies and policy differences will affect outcomes.

If government policies have contributed to the crises as argued above, then markets will respond to changes in policy. In particular, markets will reward policy clarity and punish obfuscation. Similarly, markets will punish poor, and reward good, performances by individual firms. Policies that fuzz this distinction, for example by making strong firms bear the burden of weak performance by inefficient firms, blunt the market mechanism and impede recovery.

It is fair to say that most observers have been disappointed in the response of the Thai authorities to their mounting problems. Likewise, recent moves by the South Korean government to nationalize some failing banks and industrial firms appear to be socializing risk by in effect forcing efficient South Korean firms to bear the costs of bailing out their rivals, regardless of their own capacity or culpability. In contrast, Indonesia's recent agreement with the International Monetary Fund, if implemented (and this is a big caveat) would represent a significant step towards righting Indonesian economic policy.

In this context, it is notable that among major developing countries, Thailand exhibits the largest interest rate spread between its own government bonds and US Treasury benchmark issues. And over the past year, the two countries for which the spreads have most widened are Thailand and

South Korea. In other words, the markets have been signalling their displeasure with the direction of Thai and Korean policies for the past year by demanding higher and higher rates of return on Thai and Korean sovereign debt. Indeed, last week Standard and Poor's downgraded its rating of Korean sovereign debt. (Likewise, both Moody's and Standard and Poor's have downgraded the debt ratings of a number of private banks around the region in recent weeks.)

Finally, it should be added that there may be significant spillover (as distinct from contagion) effects on other countries in the region. Trade and capital flows are the most obvious channels for the transmission of economic changes in one country to its partners. But there may be more subtle effects as well. The recent currency depreciations and credit crunches in Southeast Asia could adversely affect Vietnam, for example, by reducing its attractiveness as a host for foreign direct investment -- why build a new factory in Vietnam when one can buy (a suddenly more competitive) existing factory in Thailand for firesale prices?

IMPLICATIONS FOR THE UNITED STATES

Recent events in Asia can effect the US in a variety of ways. The most obvious has been the transmission of instability in Asian financial markets to financial markets elsewhere around the globe, including those in the United States. As the events of the past two weeks have shown, however, if the economic fundamentals are strong it is unlikely that such contagion effects could adversely effect the performance of the real economy, though the financial markets may be subject to temporary instability.

Effects on US economic performance is more likely to come through a slowdown in exports to Asia as regional growth slows. In aggregate terms, however, exports to the affected economies do not account for a significant share of US national income: taken together, exports to the developing countries of Asia account for less than 2 percent of percent of US national income, with South Korea accounting for the largest single share (around one-third of a percent of GDP). The currency devaluations will make these economies relatively more competitive in the US market. This could translate into lower prices for some imported products which could benefit US consumers, but also put pressure on domestic import-competing producers in sectors where the US continues to maintain significant domestic production. (In products such as toys, in which the US already imports nearly all of domestic consumption, the effect will be virtually a pure consumer gain.)

The recent developments in Asia also pose some challenges for US policy. It is clear that many of these economies need to significantly reform and restructure their financial systems. Deregulation does not mean no regulation, however. It would be imprudent to allow anyone with a drivers license to pilot a commercial jetliner. The financial regulators of a number of these economies are the regulatory equivalents of Sunday afternoon drivers, and soon they may be expected to fly jets. Effective regulation of modernized financial systems will require extensive (re-)training, new computers and software etc. There is enormous scope for federal, state, and private sector technical support as these countries go through their processes of reform. In the long-run, liberalization without sufficient attention to prudential regulation could prove disastrous.

At the same time, the US may also be called upon to provide financial support for reform efforts as in the recent package negotiated with Indonesia. As I argued earlier, some of the financial problems experienced in Asia are caused by politically motivated misuse of the financial system.

Ending this pattern of abuse may require going well beyond narrowly conceived technical changes and addressing fundamental issues of political reform. Governments in the region will exhibit differing degrees of capacity and willingness to undertake politically painful reforms, as confirmed by the events of recent weeks. Successful outcomes are by no means assured and as a consequence, it would be advisable to evaluate requests for financial support carefully. In this regard APEC may prove to be a useful instrument to bring peer pressure to bear on governments in the region.

August 27, 1997

ᴍEMORANDUM TO: Prime Minister Chretien

ᶠrom: Panel of Independent Experts

ˢubject: APEC Summit at Vancouver

Ve the undersigned are a panel of independent experts, composed of close observers of APEC rom most of its member economies, who are deeply committed to APEC. We applaud its mpressive progress to date and believe that it has the potential to bring substantial benefits to all ountries and peoples of the Asia Pacific region. Under your leadership, we are confident that his year's summit in Vancouver can make a major contribution toward realizing that potential.)rawing on some of the most experienced people from throughout the region, we have ssembled a set of proposals that we commend to your personal consideration as you plan and repare for Vancouver.

ᴀs you know so well, it is the annual summits that have propelled APEC so rapidly into a osition of global as well as regional prominence. Leaders decided at Blake Island to create "a ommunity of Asia Pacific economies." Leaders at Bogor committed to "achieve free and open rade in the region" by 2010/2020. Leaders at Osaka defined APEC's Action Agenda. Leaders at ˢubic last year launched the action stage and provided the critical momentum for global cceptance of the Information Technology Agreement (ITA). We believe that initiatives of imilar magnitude and impact are achievable in 1997 and recommend several for your onsideration. They would represent both timely responses to major economic developments of ecent months and commitments to achieve APEC's fundamental long-term goals.

ʰhe "Finance Summit"

ʀecent developments suggest that Vancouver should focus on achieving financial security for the egion. Our proposals would in fact enable APEC to make a major contribution to resolving ome of the most pressing problems facing the world financial system as well as the region itself- replicating in the monetary area APEC's success in simultaneously pursuing its regional and lobal trade objectives.

ᴀPEC Ministers have already agreed to make a major push to achieve worldwide agreement on iberalization of financial services in the WTO. An APEC agreement on the issue in November vould almost certainly galvanize a global accord by the target date of December 12. Successful ᴀPEC leadership on financial services in 1997 would thus replicate its role on the ITA in 1996. ʰhis achievement alone would assure a positive worldwide reaction to Vancouver.

As with the ITA, however, success can be achieved only with skillful negotiation of an agreement that meets the interests of all major APEC members. In particular, several of the key Asian developing countries must commit to more extensive opening and modernization of their financial markets. While they recognize that such movement is necessary to achieve the agreed goal of financing growth, their willingness to do so has been jeopardized by the currency crises in the region. These crises have thus jeopardized the core of the liberalization strategy for 1997, based on bringing the financial services talks to a successful conclusion, and they therefore threaten the success of the Vancouver summit itself.

We believe that Leaders can take two steps that will simultaneously save the financial services effort and, more importantly, launch a major new avenue of APEC cooperation. First, Leaders must articulate the reality that the currency crises *increase*, rather than detract from, the need for reform of financial sectors in affected countries and others that might be hit in the future. Weak financial sectors are a central cause of the present currency problems, as they were in Mexico and elsewhere in Latin America in 1995. No country can restore market and worldwide confidence unless it greatly strengthens that sector. The United States was forced to learn that lesson in the 1980s, Japan is pursuing its own "big bang" liberalization program today, Korea is struggling to launch one, and the rest of the region from Mexico to Indonesia must do so as well.

Liberalization and deregulation, as called for in the WTO negotiations, are thus essential to the restoration of stability and economic growth in the region -- the ultimate goals of APEC cooperation. However, adequate supervisory regimes must accompany these reforms. This will take both time and technical assistance. The United States and others must therefore accept longer phase-in periods for the reforms. In addition, they must help the liberalizing countries install effective systems of prudential regulation and supervision. An APEC agreement on financial services should thus include a generous component of economic and technical cooperation (ecotech in APEC terminology), as well as liberalization, thereby strengthening the most neglected dimension of the APEC process and adding to the case for a major APEC initiative on the issue.

A second, even bolder, financial initiative could complement the national sectoral reforms and assure that Vancouver would rank as the most innovative APEC summit since Bogor. We believe that APEC should respond to the deep concerns experienced throughout the region over the current currency turmoil, including Prime Minister Mahathir's public indication that he intends to raise the issue at Vancouver and President Suharto's renewed call for APEC "to create a common safety network" in his National Day speech on August 16, by creating new mechanisms to supplement those of the International Monetary Fund to help prevent such crises in the future and provide additional funding for those that do occur.

In response to initiatives that you launched at the G-7 summit in Halifax, the IMF has improved both its "early warning" and financing capabilities. However, the preventive system failed again in Thailand. Contagion again spread to other countries. The new IMF financing arrangements did not prove usable so the support package once again had to be cobbled together on an ad hoc basis.

APEC could provide two crucial complements to the IMF procedures. First, it could deploy its evolving system of "peer pressure" or "positive encouragement" to help persuade countries to take preemptive action. Countries in trouble might be more inclined to accept unwelcome advice from community neighbors than from the IMF (let alone the G-7 or one or two large powers acting alone). The neighbors would have a legitimate case for providing such advice because, as recent events indicate, they can be severely injured if timely action is not taken. The APEC Finance Ministers have already discussed these issues and would be a natural venue for such an effort.

Second, APEC governments and central banks could provide a new financing facility to augment IMF programs in the region. As with Thailand now and Mexico in 1995, the IMF itself cannot supply nearly enough funding to enable countries to effectively defend their new (and politically difficult) adjustment programs. An APEC Supplementary Financing Facility would strengthen the ability of the IMF to persuade countries to adopt needed reforms, enhance the confidence of troubled countries that they could sustain the needed reforms, and provide a dramatic indicator of regional solidity.

Such a "Chretien Fund" could make a major contribution to both international financial stability and to APEC. It would also greatly strengthen the prospect for successful completion of the negotiations on financial sector reform by assuring countries in the region of additional help if such reform were to trigger future problems (as some of them fear). It would stamp Vancouver as the "finance summit." Leaders at Vancouver could direct their Finance Ministers to work out the details, as you and your G-7 colleagues did at Halifax in beginning to erect the essential (but still inadequate) improvements in the IMF system to deal with "future Mexicos".

<u>Trade Liberalization</u>

Trade liberalization and reform continue to be central objectives of APEC. The Bogor targets and the ITA, on which Leaders played the decisive role, are the organization's most notable achievements. It is essential to maintain the movement toward realizing the free trade commitments; the Bogor targets will quickly lose credibility once any APEC summit fails to do so, and the world will be quick to criticize any such outcome.

<u>Sectoral liberalization</u> now appears a most promising route to rapid progress. Financial services liberalization, as described above, would represent a further major step in this direction. In addition, your Trade Ministers and officials have been developing a list of additional candidates for sectoral reform and the member countries have already nominated a rich list of possibilities.

We recommend that leaders make a commitment at Vancouver to achieve agreements in three or four additional sectors over the next year or two, thereby assuring sustained momentum toward achieving the Bogor targets and providing convincing evidence of APEC's willingness to fulfill its pledges. It will not be enough to simply designate one or two sectors for exploratory negotiations. Firm commitments to actually reach new agreements are required, as with the Bogor targets themselves. The nature of the agreements will of course differ from sector to sector: some, like the ITA, may include elimination of all tariffs; some may go further, to address nontariff measures as well; while some may only, at least in an initial stage, harmonize standards and other facilitation steps.

Four criteria could govern the selection of specific sectors. One is of course their economic significance; it would be advantageous to liberalize sectors that will bring sizable benefits to APEC economies. A second is the risk they pose of future trade conflict; APEC should make every effort to prevent future disputes by anticipatory liberalization and facilitation. A third criterion is the balance of members' interests; it will be especially important to include sectors of benefit to developing member countries. A final key variable is the existence of industry support; as demonstrated in the case of the ITA, this greatly smoothes the intergovernmental effort and subsequent domestic approval of APEC agreements. Attached is an illustrative list of eleven sectoral candidates that seem to meet these tests, though we would not claim to have yet had time to subject them (or other nominated sectors) to any rigorous analysis or screening process.

APEC can also now consolidate its <u>leadership of the global trading system</u>. In addition to galvanizing additional sectoral agreements, it should promote globalization of the Bogor commitments by starting to seek agreement in the WTO on a goal of global free trade by 2010/2020. Such an "APEC challenge" would promote achievement of the region's own liberalization goals in a manner fully consistent with its multilateral trade objectives. The goal could be pursued by APEC Trade Ministers at the WTO Ministerial Conferences in 1998 and/or 2000 for progress toward a new "APEC Round".

Leaders should also agree to order <u>a comprehensive review of the first decade of APEC</u> achievements in 1999. This review would assess progress to date on trade liberalization, facilitation, and economic and technical cooperation and point the way for future action. The review could give substance to the "APEC challenge" to nonmembers on trade liberalization and other APEC agenda issues. To assure its objectivity and utility for Leaders, an independent task force from outside official circles should be commissioned to conduct the review.

<u>Economic and Technical Cooperation (ecotech)</u>

APEC places high priority on ecotech and its central role in building an Asia Pacific community. The principles for successful ecotech were laid out at Manila but implementation to date has been highly fragmented and largely ineffectual. Better management is needed but devising a clear strategic focus is far more important.

One approach is to aggressively employ ecotech in support of APEC's trade liberalization and facilitation agenda by improving administrative cooperation and transferring technology and best practices. At the same time, liberalization and facilitation will open areas conventionally earmarked for the public sector to the private sector, with incentives, as in the building of public infrastructure.

In many sectors, ecotech is in fact an essential complement of liberalization if the benefits of the latter are to be maximized. For example:

- bank supervisors need to be trained to implement financial sector reform;

- educational institutions need to be linked electronically to maximize the benefits of the new information technologies (and thus the ITA);

- testing and certification labs and technicians will be needed to administer harmonization of auto emission and noise abatement standards, the likely starting points of an auto sector agreement;

- technicians must be trained and facilities built to take advantage of the expanded availability of medical equipment if that sector is liberalized.

We thus recommend that the Vancouver summit stress the potential benefits of ecotech, note that it can greatly enhance the gains from trade liberalization and facilitation, and direct Ministers and officials to develop projects that will take full advantage of such linkages.

Environmental Issues

Both the developed and developing economies within APEC have a deep interest in efficient solutions to global environment problems.

An essential element in a solution to the problem of greenhouse gas emissions must be the efficient location of energy industries and efficient specialization in energy trade within the APEC region, consistent with APEC economies realizing their full development potential without damage to the global environment.

The European proposals for uniform reductions of carbon emissions by all Annex I countries run counter to this APEC objective.

In the leadup to the Kyoto Conference, APEC leaders could usefully underline their commitment to solutions to the environment problem caused by greenhouse gas emissions and call for solutions which encourage efficient reduction of carbon emissions by (1) eliminating existing distortions in energy markets, (2) calling for the formulation of a system which achieves reductions while minimizing economic costs and (3) transferring technologies that promote clean and efficient energy use.

Conclusion

The potential agenda for Vancouver is very rich. We believe that some combination of the suggested initiatives could make it the most successful APEC summit to date. We commend them to you attention and would be delighted to elaborate or discuss them further if you would like to do so.

C. Fred Bergsten, United States
Chia Siow Yue, Singapore
Wendy Dobson, Canada
Peter Drysdale, Australia
Jesus Estanislao, Philippines
Ralph Lattimore, New Zealand
Suhadi Mankusuwondo, Indonesia
Luis Rubio, Mexico
Suthiphand Chirathivat, Thailand
Rong-I Wu, Chinese Taipei
Ippei Yamazawa, Japan
Soogil Young, Korea
Zhang Yunling, China

Attachment

SECTORAL AGREEMENT CANDIDATES FOR VANCOUVER

Sector (country sponsors)	Comments
1. Agriculture (Australia)	WTO negotiations to resume 2000; APEC could catalyze as with ITA 1996 and financial services 1997. Oilseeds could represent first installment in 1998. Agreement to immediately replace all nontariff measures with tariffs and bind agricultural protection would be useful first steps.
2. Automobiles and parts (US)	World's largest manufacturing sector. Huge inefficiencies exist throughout Asia due to high protection. Major disputes. Could start by harmonizing emissions and noise abatement standards.
3. Chemicals (Korea, US)	Basic industrial building block (like ITA). Many national industries want liberalization and have jointly developed a four-stage program.
4. Civil aviation	Build on expanding number of bilateral agreements to promote regional "open skies" accord.
5. Energy/energy equipment (Australia, New Zealand, Thailand)	Basic commodities with major economy-wide and environmental implications.
6. Environmental goods/services (Canada, Japan, Taiwan, US)	Would help support more efficient environmental policies.
7. Fish/ fish products (Brunei, Canada, Thailand, New Zealand)	Major export interest of several smaller countries.
8. Medical equipment (Singapore, Thailand, US)	Upgrade medical care and reduce costs.
9. Textiles and apparel (Indonesia)	Chief manufactured export of many developing countries.
10. Toys (China and Hong Kong)	Key Chinese interest. Almost agreed in Uruguay Round.
11. Steel (Korea)	Basic industrial building block. A nondiscriminatory APEC steel agreement could include technical assistance, raw materials supply assurances and new financing facilities.

○

APEX
TP
9780160563911
76901945 — 23